Because I am

Christian accompaniment through the experience of
a pre-birth diagnosis of a possible disability

PARISH RESOURCE

Published by Redemptorist Publications
Wolf's Lane, Chawton, Hampshire, GU34 3HQ, UK
Tel. +44 (0)1420 88222, Fax. +44 (0)1420 88805
Email rp@rpbooks.co.uk, www.rpbooks.co.uk

A registered charity limited by guarantee
Registered in England 3261721

Text by Cristina Gangemi
Edited by Peter Edwards
Designed by Eliana Thompson
Photos/illustrated by Stefania Prendelli

ISBN 978-0-85231-528-6

A CIP catalogue record for this book is available from the British Library

The publisher gratefully acknowledges permission to use the following copyright material:

Excerpts from *The Jerusalem Bible*, copyright © 1966 by Darton, Longman & Todd, Ltd and Doubleday, a division of Random House, Inc. Reprinted by permission.

Excerpts from the *New Revised Standard Version Bible: Anglicised Edition*, copyright © 1989. 1995, Division of Christian Education of the National Council of the Churches of Christ in the United States of America. Used by permission. All rights reserved.

Every effort has been made to trace copyright holders and to obtain their permission for the use of copyright material. The publisher apologises for any errors or omissions and would be grateful for notification of any corrections that should be incorporated in future reprints or editions of this book.

Printed by Lithgo Press Ltd.,
Leicester, LE8 6NU

Because I am

Christian accompaniment through the experience of
a pre-birth diagnosis of a possible disability

Cristina Gangemi
Illustrations by Stefania Prandelli

PARISH RESOURCE

redemptorist
p u b l i c a t i o n s

Dedication

This book is dedicated to the three people whose story called me to write this resource: to Karl, Ewelina and Plamen, thank you for sharing your love and journey with me.

And to Becky, Gerard, Aurelia, Claudio, Charlotte, Giorgio and Monsignor Jim, thank you.

For the
wonder
of who
I am

CONTENTS

FOREWORD

by Cardinal Gianfranco Ravasi

In 1994 an academic, Nancy Eiesland, who had lived with an experience of physical disability, published a wise text entitled *The Disabled God*, in which she proposed a possible theology of disability. Her research traced the cry of the ancient biblical patriarch Jacob and his protest-dialogue with a God who seemed both loving and cruel. However, from within her own cry she proposed a radical metamorphosis based upon the Christian faith, where the crucified Christ resides at its centre, its prayer and its belief. Jean Vanier, the founder of L'Arche, now spread throughout the world, well expressed this spiritual vision, "Mine is not faith in a powerful God, but in a powerful God who became vulnerable, impoverished so as to join us in our own human weaknesses."

This was similar to the intuitive thought of the theologian Dietrich Bonhoeffer, martyred by the Nazis in 1945, and who, without hesitation, noted that in the Flossenbürg concentration camp, "God, in Christ, saves us not in the virtue of his omnipotence but in his impotence." In suffering and death the human person can be identified and it is also in this that the Son of God becomes fully our brother. Jesus Christ is wonderfully human and marvellously divine: this image is often found in Byzantine icons where he is presented as resurrected, glorious and *Pantokrator*, that is omnipotent, but still with the signs of his passion and crucifixion. This is a theological background that can pastorally accompany, on one hand, the parents and their child who is differently able and, on the other, the parish community, so that they might know how to accompany and gather these families deep into their being, that they might be close to Christ in his living and in his suffering.

The *Because I Am* texts are the fruit of a seminar, sponsored by the Pontifical Council for Culture, which took place in the Vatican on 23 June 2016 and which produced a "declaration of principles" under the name of the Living Fully charter.

This statement, its perspective and general approach, is founded on and dedicated to life. It presents in all human people a life that has, within itself, the seeds of transcendence and a native dignity, which is to be respected but most of all gathered together and celebrated. This, of course, does not exclude the understanding and closeness that must be shown to parents who have to face, sometimes dramatically, such a demanding experience. They are to be sustained, accompanied and guided without moralising, or pietism, but with realism and trust, in a true and personal process of elaboration, formation and growth.

We can, therefore, consider the *BIA* parents' resource as a map of a human and spiritual journey which can take place, firstly with parents who have children with serious experiences of disability, often diagnosed before birth. They form an itinerary of reflections upon the events, the questions and the problematic knots that present themselves to parents living this life experience, beginning with the unexpected nature of their pregnancy. Alongside such parents, as they travel, other parents, who have already travelled along similar paths, are involved that they might be effective witnesses and authentic partners for their journey.

Naturally, a thematic guide, which moves within such a complex horizon, must be underpinned by a solid theological foundation, one which begins from a profound concept of the body and of life in all its fullness. The human creation, in fact, is not only a biological structure but also a personal reality for which no therapy or appeal to psychology, while necessary, is sufficient; it requires understanding and human closeness, a support which is spiritual and also loving. It is exactly because we are mostly turned towards parents of faith – without excluding those who may be searching and "provoked" by their difficult experience – that this text includes a diary with reflections and prayers.

• • •

The *BIA* parish resource points us, in contrast, directly to the Christian community, in particular to parishes, in the form of a pastoral programme. It is based upon the previously mentioned Living Fully charter's "declaration of principles" and it is rich in guidelines and suggestions for all the faithful so that they might, in some way, share the hopes and sufferings of the parents who are involved in such difficult journeys.

Because I Am is, therefore, a journey that the community undertakes in the company of the parents, from the moment of pre-birth diagnosis, offering them the light that comes from the word of God and the message that the Church gives. This can be heard, especially, from the impassioned voice of Pope Francis, who sends them the warmth of ecclesial and pastoral accompaniment. In this way, positive horizons can open up before the parents' eyes and that of their families, which can bloom from their children, no matter what their strength, weakness or condition may be. When lived with the loving presence of the community, this experience can be transformed, revealing unexpected aspects and colours, which have surprising outcomes.

Often, in fact, the parents of children who are intellectually disabled suffer from terrible solitude, in which they feel isolated as they meet their sometimes challenging vocation. It is here that we note the importance of "transforming vulnerability, oftentimes limited and extreme, into a life of true communion", as expressed by the French philosopher Julia Kristeva, who encountered the reality of L'Arche, was cited by Jean Vanier and whose own son, David, lived with a serious neurological condition. Supportive parish groups, therefore, can be born where networks are developed and where dialogue between families with similar concerns might flower from sharing stories. One can discover the greatness of a human person, who, while fragile, can identify with the "Disabled God", knowing their dignity for one simple matter of fact: *Just because I am.* In his discourse given in the Brazilian shrine of Aparecida on 24 July 2013, Pope Francis turned towards a world of suffering, much like the experiences we have underlined, affirming that "The Church is not far from your struggles, but we accompany you with affection. The Lord is close to you and holds you by the hand. Look towards him in the most difficult moments and he will give you consolation and hope."

• • •

In addition to the texts of this precious and significant project, I would like to leave the last word to a parent who has lived the same experience as parents to whom we dedicate this resource. It is that of the French philosopher Emmanuel Mounier (1905–50), whose daughter Françoise was born with acute encephalitis and seemed to live in a place from which she could not emerge. Her father wrote, in his diary, a strong and courageous witness to faith. Not all people can carry such a spiritually intense vocation, through which they can be renewed and testify. We, however, can hear his trustful voice of fellowship in times of trial:

> "What sense would all of this have if our child was only a body that was impaired, or a bit of life that was painful, and not, instead, a small white host that surpasses us all, an immense mystery of love which would dazzle us if we saw it face to face? We must not think of pain as something that is ripped from us but something that we surrender to the little Christ whom we find in our midst… I have felt the sensation as I draw close to her small bed, without a voice, to be drawing close to an altar, to a sacred space where God speaks through a sign. We had wished that Françoise would die, is this not sentimentalism? what does it mean for her to be disgraced? who says that she is so? Maybe we have been asked to safeguard and to adore a host, in the midst of us. My little Françoise, you are, for me, an image of faith."

Card. Ravasi

Cardinal Gianfranco Ravasi

INTRODUCTION

Meeting our story

Over the years I have been asked to support parishes and families as they live out their lives of faith and share their stories with others. One day, in 2016, I was asked to support a couple who had received the news that the child they were expecting was diagnosed with a medical condition and might experience a disability. I was honoured to be asked to accompany them on their journey. I have always been struck by the lack of resources and advice that is available to Christian parents who find themselves upon this unexpected, painful and frightening pathway. Many of these parents, as my colleague Professor John Wyatt would say, enter into "human dilemmas in the light of [their] Christian faith",[1] concerning issues of life and death. I believe that experience provides an invaluable source for responding to pastoral needs. Providing pastoral support, from within the Christian tradition, "begins as we confront urgent concerns [and] pressing issues"[2] that arise from personal experience. As I accompanied this family, through urgent, difficult but loving times, I asked myself what my own experience could bring to their life and journey. There seem to be three distinct, personal experiences that I feel allowed me to share with them. I have shared a lived experience.

My own life is an example of a challenging, pre-birth medical condition. When I was conceived, I was a member of a set of triplets who went on a very different journey. Two of my fertilised siblings, instead of travelling towards the womb, went into a fallopian tube and began to grow there but they did not survive; they became ectopic pregnancies. I for some reason travelled into the womb and began to grow. My mother became very ill and underwent a life-saving operation, which removed the embryos who did not survive. I, growing safely, was moved to one side while this operation took place – you could say I was put aside while decisions were made about my life and my mother's. It was only when I was preparing for this resource that my mother began to tell me about how difficult it was for her. She shared about the time that she had spent with the priest deciding what she should do in case of death. My mother told me that the prayers of the priest, before she went for the operation, helped her to prepare for my eventual death, which most of the doctors had assured her would occur. Suddenly, I began to think even more deeply about my ministries with families and with disabled people as I realised that it was also my own personal story. I know that life is a gift because I was truly given that gift and as such I am able to speak with some empathy about the life of an unborn baby in a vulnerable position.

The second experience moves from my own story in the womb to that of my grandson's. Giorgio was diagnosed with a medical condition named VACTERL association, the effect of which is a short limb and some difficulties in swallowing, as his oesophagus was attached to his lung and not his stomach, and he had club feet. This condition was diagnosed at his twelve-week scan. As doctors helped my son and daughter-in-law to understand their child's medical needs, they, like many parents, were faced with many questions. Professionals and others presented them with information that asked them to think about whether Giorgio's life had the same value as a baby who did not have VACTERL association. My son Claudio, a teacher of Religious Education, and daughter-in-law Charlotte were suddenly on a pathway that involved heart-wrenching thoughts, considerations and decisions about the baby, whom they had conceived as a companion in their life, as a sign of their deep love for one another. Suddenly, as I heard the news about Giorgio, my own story came back to me, my own time in the womb. All the words I had ever thought or written concerning disability and the human person were part of my very own story again. I was also preparing a large symposium and conference in Rome called "Living Fully 2016", which promoted the important, gift-filled existence of disabled people in the world. We were going to Rome to celebrate the lives of disabled people. At the same time, at home, the story of my very own grandson was bringing to life all the conversations we were about to have. Most people presumed that I would be able to support my son through the knowledge that I had built up over the years. I was warned against making my own theological position concerning disability override the choices they had to make about the viability of Giorgio's life. These were indeed presumptions for, as a mother and grandmother, that was not my role. I was called to accompany, sharing information about what the Christian Church taught, when I was asked. In answer to many questions they had I was able to gently place at the service of my family the voices of many Christians who, over the span of millennia, had thought about and planned for the very life-changing decisions and dilemmas that now faced their lives. My role was not to tell them what to do. It was to love them and *to be with* them as they tried to discover how they could, in a grace-filled way, be guided by the love they felt for their child and themselves. After much sharing, talking, thinking and questioning, they decided to go forward and carry Giorgio's life to term, not knowing fully what to expect.

On the night that he was born, he underwent a four-hour operation, before which my son, accompanied gently by his wife and the nurses in the neo-natal department, administered the rite of baptism under a state of emergency. These were four agonising hours of waiting, reminding me of what it must have been like for Christ, praying in the garden of Gethsemane as the possibility of his death approached. All we could do was to follow Christ's example: to pray and to wait. Giorgio is now one and a half years old and is our gift. Following many months in hospital he has learnt to use his shorter arm naturally and lives each day managing his food. He is most definitely the presence of grace in our life. It has not been an easy road and we have endured many moments of anxiety along the way, but we have also noted the moments where God's touch has been part of our journey; we have had many lessons

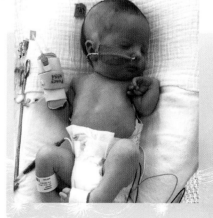

about what love is. It was only in this experience that all of my words, the books I have read and the Christian approach to the human person made sense; they all came into being, in the human *being* of Giorgio. This has helped me even further, as I have been called to accompany other parents and parishes through this experience; Giorgio has become my teacher.

Each family's situation has been different, and each life has travelled a different path, but accompaniment and thinking through with love has enabled each family to know what is possible with God. Following these experiences, I have realised, even further, the urgent need for parents to be accompanied when faced with anxieties and dilemmas surrounding a pre-birth diagnosis of a medical condition or possible disability. The *Because I Am (BIA)* journey is, therefore, designed to provide a response to this urgent pastoral need. It has emerged from the gentle teaching of Giorgio and the three families who accompany this resource. I do not tell their stories but you will find their words interwoven throughout the accompanying parents' resource.

As we move now into the body of the *BIA* journey of parish formation, let me end this section by inviting you to meet another, very important person. A man called John Oliver has provided me with the most insightful lesson for my work and ministry. I was interviewing people with intellectual disabilities for my research project in 2009, "EveryBody Has a Story",[3] which explored spirituality and religious practice with people who experience intellectual disabilities. One of our interviewees was John Oliver, whose welcome always involved opening doors and leading us in as we arrived. John was a creative communicator, choosing to use certain sentences and symbols to share his story. We were exploring the "big questions" about life: "Why am I here? What can I do? Where do I find love?" and so on. These were deep questions about our lives, our spirits and God. When we had started the focus groups it had been suggested that John Oliver might not find the correct words to answer such questions, but we felt it important to give him the choice to respond if he wished to.

The session progressed, and we noticed that he was watching the symbols, pictures, words and signs that we used to ask our big questions. When it was John Oliver's turn, through the use of symbols and the spoken word we asked him. "John Oliver, why do you think you are in this world?" Generally, he chose not to communicate through words but, on this occasion, he looked me straight in the eye, totally bemused by my question, and said, "Because I am!" It was as simple as that. I feel he was wondering *why* I had asked that question, as if I was waiting for some sort of justification for his existence. John Oliver taught me that we can never know why a person exists and that everyone should be accepted, just because they are. It is with this insight from John Oliver that I now invite you into the *Because I Am* journey.

As you travel, individually and as a parish group, you will be asked to reflect a little on what you have read and shared. Each section of the book carries activities for you to complete. We hope that these activities will help you to set up a *BIA* group of accompaniers in your parish community.

CHAPTER ONE

THE *BECAUSE I AM* JOURNEY

TRAVELLING WITH GRACE;
GETTING TO KNOW THE STORY

What is the *Because I Am (BIA)* journey?

The *BIA* journey is a programme of reflection and spiritual accompaniment for parents whose child receives a pre-birth diagnosis of a medical condition or possible experience of disability. It provides a reflective journey into the issues that face Christian parents and their unborn child in such life experiences. The journey includes reflections from parents who have travelled similar paths along with insights from culture and the Christian tradition. It is a journey of Christian accompaniment.

The *BIA* resources cannot cover every pastoral situation that may arise. The *BIA* approach advocates that accompaniment should enable Christians to respond to people's needs no matter their particular situation. This can also include supporting families who experience disability as a result of a difficult or problematic birth. The underpinning principles of the *BIA* programme pay a focused attention to the life and voice of the child. They allow for a deeper understanding that all people, no matter their ability, are valued members of our lives and held in the love of God. These principles will guide our journey.

What is the *BIA* approach?

BIA pays careful and loving attention to the story of unborn children and their parent(s) through the lens of Christian teaching. It does not seek to advise parents on what to do but to accompany them in a way that is accurate and informed. The BIA approach takes "EveryBody's"[4] story into consideration, ensuring that the voice of the child is included when decisions are being made about his or her life and potential. *BIA* is deeply Christian. It is non-judgemental, providing the space and tools for "breathing with God".

13

The following principles underpin the *BIA* approach:

- It is a pastoral accompaniment that is never based on judgements; it is non-judgemental.

- It recognises and acknowledges that all life is gift and that no life is without value.

- It invites and encourages a parish to develop a *BIA* team of pastoral accompaniers who can support families through pre-birth diagnosis, pregnancy, palliative care and experiences of disability.

- It is an act of empathy whereby we do not project our own beliefs into a story but accompany people, sharing our faith with them through loving witness. In this way we are sharing our beliefs together.

- It pays particular attention to the vocation, purpose and presence of the unborn child.

- It engages the reader/parish/parents in faith-filled reading of scripture.

- It supports families by recognising their anxieties and looking to the future.

- It assures parents and children they are not alone, giving the parish and their family tools for accompaniment.

- It provides information for parish/parents concerning Christian teaching on the human person.

- It invites parents and parish to pray with the child and with God and to notice moments of grace. We have named these "*scintilli* of grace".[5]

- It invites parents/parishes to recognise moments of grace as they journey, based on love.

Who are the *BIA* parents?

The BIA parents are the families whose stories are at the foundation of the *BIA* resources. Their stories are shared throughout the books and their pathways have formed support and pastoral accompaniment. They are the people who have gently, and with love, provided the peer support for the parents you are called to accompany.

What are the *BIA* resources?

1. An interactive resource book for parents;

2. A prayer diary to accompany *BIA*;

3. A parish resource, which includes a programme of formation for parish communities.

The *BIA* journey parents' resources: some information

BIA parents' book

As parents encounter moments in their life that are both emotional and challenging, the interactive parents' resource *Because I Am* (BIA), together with the *BIA* prayer diary, will provide them with a way of stopping, reflecting and breathing with God. *BIA* provides loving and honest pathways for parents to reflect upon, based on the wisdom and stories of people who have travelled a parallel road. At a time when the human and spiritual potential of the child is placed entirely into the hands of others, this resource will also seek to enable the child's voice, purpose and story to be present, because the child, too, is on the journey with his or her parents.

BIA prayer diary

The *BIA* prayer diary accompanies the *BIA* parents' book. It will give parents space to record and remember their thoughts, emotions, hopes and challenges. Mostly it will help parents to pray and reflect. In the past I have found that the pathways that they travel will be times of soul-searching and that having space to reflect is helped by a place to write and draw their experiences. Parents are encouraged to use the diary and pray at the end of each chapter.

The *BIA* journey: what will I have to do?

The *BIA* parish resource invites parish communities to practise Christian accompaniment through genuine love of neighbour. Following a pre-birth diagnosis of disability, parents and their unborn child find themselves on an unexpected pathway. The most common emotions expressed at this time are usually ones of fear and loss. Parents comment that it can often be a time of great loneliness where they begin to feel a sense of difference or, at the very worst, they mistakenly feel punished. The *BIA* programme of parish accompaniment will help you support families. It will provide you with the pastoral tools that you will need to share with them as they travel on a journey with their child. Christian solidarity is based on the genuine practice of love, which can be given by making a commitment to accompany them as they travel. Through dedicating your time and attention to this serious and urgent pastoral need, you will be responding to a call to holiness. In his apostolic exhortation *Gaudete et Exsultate*, "On the Call to Holiness in Today's World",[6] Pope Francis reminds us: "We are all called to be holy by living our lives with love and by bearing witness in everything we do, wherever we find ourselves." When you find yourself accompanying parents, along unexpected pathways, you ensure that there is a place for them to rest, to share and to know that they are not alone. You stand on holy ground and witness to the presence of grace in people's lives. The *BIA* journey will help you live this important ministry.

How does the *BIA* journey begin? *BIA* start-points

The *BIA* journey can begin with: a request for help from a parent or parishioner; a parent who is in urgent need of support; the desire of the parish to be prepared should parents need support; the request of a church leader; a person who has been disabled or a parent who wishes to share his or her story and support others. The *BIA* journey has three separate *BIA* start-points:

- Proactive parish/chaplaincy development (disability awareness);

- Programme of formation for Christian accompaniment;

- Plan for responding to an urgent/immediate request for accompaniment; we name this the Immediate Response Strategy (IRS).

What is an Immediate Response Strategy (IRS)?

When parents ask for help and guidance following a pre-birth diagnosis for their child, the pastor must react immediately to support the family and should activate the IRS. The parents begin to travel along an unexpected pathway and will need immediate accompaniment and informed, non-judgemental guidance. This may mean that you do not have time to initiate an in-depth programme of *BIA* formation and will need to make an immediate response. In such cases you should turn to chapter 4 and carefully read though "Start-point 3" on p. 78. This will help you respond quickly and support parents immediately.

These start-points can be initiated as a whole programme of parish development, using all three stages in succession or merging some of the directives from each stage. They can be used together or individually, according to need. They have been designed to allow you to accompany the unborn child and his or her parents in a way that is immediate and authentic and in a way that will provide lasting change for your parish or chaplaincy service.

The *BIA* parish resource

This resource introduces the *BIA* journey and its tools while inviting you to do the following:

- Form a parish team and engage with the *BIA* parish resource, following the activities it sets out for you to follow.

- Read sections of the *BIA* parents' resource. This resource will give you the information and language that you will need as you encourage parents to breathe with God and notice moments of grace as they travel.

- Dedicate time to accompanying parents and assisting them in finding networks of support and information about services that might help them in their lives.

- Work with your parish team and pastor to ensure that couples are accompanied in times of great pain. This may include accompanying as they face the death of their child.

- Welcome and celebrate the life of a child who is born with a possible experience of disability, ensuring that his or her place of belonging is both affirmed and celebrated in practice.

Each chapter in this *BIA* parish resource will give you activities to follow: some will be reading sections of the parents' book, some will invite you to engage in personal reflection; and some will be group activities. Please do take time to complete each activity. Thank you for your time and the witness that you give to Christian love.

BIA journey: a note from the author concerning "Method in Ministry"[7]

The *BIA* journey has been developed as a "portable method" of pastoral accompaniment and prayerful reflection. As parents make hospital visits, spend time alone or reflect and share with others, we hope that the *BIA* journey will help them and you to recognise and respond to God's saving presence through words, prayers and images.

We will do this by following the MEET process that I developed in 2006 specifically for the purpose of exploring, accessing and mediating on issues of faith and life. It will provide you with structure as you read through the *BIA* journey.

MEET = Meet, Explain, **Explore**, Transcend

This process must be used in partnership with the parents' resource book

Using the MEET method to navigate your way through the *BIA* parish resource

M: Meet the pastoral context, the possible experience that parents may encounter as their unborn child receives a pre-birth diagnosis of a medical condition or possible disability. Meet the *BIA* journey, its approach, resources and purpose. Meet some of the issues that surround the life of disabled people within the human story. You will also meet Christian teaching surrounding the dignity of life. You will be directed to read chapters 2 and 4 from the *BIA* parents' resource. (Introduction, chapters 1 and 2 of *BIA* parish resource.)

E: Explain the four *BIA* pathways and advice offered to parents in the *BIA* parents' resource. This will provide you with knowledge for your time of accompaniment. This will require individual, or collective, reading of chapter 6 in the *BIA* parents' resource. You will be asked to spend time in reflection with your parish team and make plans to put your learning into action. (Chapter 3 of *BIA* parish resource.)

E: Explore how to run a *BIA* project in your parish. The practice of Christian accompaniment: listening and attending with love. This will require you to recruit a parish team and discuss how you might develop a team of accompaniers in your parish. This can work at different levels according to pastoral need. It will require you to activate all that you have learnt and how you begin will depend on the urgency of your pastoral need. (Chapter 4 of *BIA* parish resource.)

T: Transcend – *BIA* in practice: begin to run a programme in your parish, accompanying parents as they move through and beyond the pain of pre-birth diagnosis. Help parents notice moments of grace and mark the wonder of who they and their child are. (Chapter 5 of *BIA* parish resource.)

Extra reading for deeper insight

Chapters 1, 3 and 5 of the *BIA* parents' resource provide an imaginative retelling of the pre-birth journey of the Christ child. This also attends to the unexpected journey of the people who had been chosen to accompany his life as parents. To run a *BIA* journey, it is not necessary for you to read these chapters but they may provide you with some further insights for your accompaniment. These chapters were written to help parents enter into an empathic journey with Christ and his human story. However, I would highly recommend that you give some time to this imaginative retelling of stories from the Christian tradition in the case of parents choosing to share some reflections with you. It is also a creative way to enter into the experience of unexpected journeys and the stories of *BIA* parents, whose experiences have accompanied the development of the *BIA* journey.

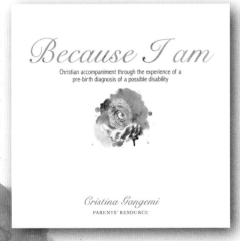

Because I am

Christian accompaniment through the experience of a pre-birth diagnosis of a possible disability

Cristina Gangemi

PARENTS' RESOURCE

The MEET process will be a framework that we will use to help people to share stories, in a way that is natural and non-intrusive. It is designed to enable faith communities to share stories from tradition, culture and experience. In times of great suffering, its structure will help you to notice *scintilli*: moments of grace in challenging times. I hope that, by using it as a method for sharing in a family's story, it will help you to recognise *scintilli* in your own life. In this way you can bring your own faith into conversations with the culture of the parish, the experiences of the parents and their unborn child as well as the richness of Christian tradition.

In summary

Instructions for using the *BIA* parish resource and preparing for the *BIA* journey

M: Read through the introduction, chapter 1 and chapter 2. Follow directives (this section is preparatory and will require a lot of reading time). Alternatively you could invite two people to read and develop a summary presentation.

E: Read through chapter 3 – here we explain the four *BIA* pathways and invite you to follow directives.

E: Read through chapter 4, explore the *BIA* formation structure and choose the stage you will begin your *BIA* journey, follow directives.

T: Read through chapter 5, make plans for activating *BIA* in your setting and at your chosen stage.

Some chapters provide moments of *BIA* formation. They include formative reflections from the author and *BIA* parents and activities to undertake. These are named "*scintilli*" or "activity" boxes. They are designed to inform your *BIA* journeys and encourage you to notice God's touch.

In this chapter we have introduced you to the *BIA* journey, inviting you to meet its approach, methods, tools and underpinning principles. In chapter 2 we will continue to meet the *BIA* approach, focusing on the rich Christian traditions surrounding the life of the unborn child. We meet the wonder of who we are.

As we begin to enter into the *BIA* journey, we invite you to pray.

We pray that your accompaniment will give parents some peace and hope and that our images and words may inform your *BIA* journey. As you begin this ministry, Please take some time to breathe with God, and notice moments of grace as you prepare to accompany others.

CHAPTER TWO

MEETING THE CONTEXT
AN UNEXPECTED JOURNEY

"For the wonder of who I am, I praise you."

(based on Psalm 139:14)

This line, from Psalm 139, has been a constant inspiration over the past twenty years, during which time I have worked as a disability adviser. It has been a privileged journey where I have met and accompanied many disabled people and their families, as they have sought to live out their lives and faith. During this time, I have spoken with many parents whose children have been disabled by a complex and generally inaccessible world. Parents have shared their stories about their child's journey to birth. Together we have spent honoured moments, remembering the pathways on which they found themselves. We have all agreed that they were times of "great love, anxiety, pain, prayer and expectations". In such times, encouraging people to remain in God's presence, know the wonder of who they are and feel God's hand in their life has always been at the centre of the pastoral support I have sought to share.

When parents receive the news that their unborn child has a medical condition and may experience disability, it is usually a time of great anxiety. Parents begin to feel different from their peers; they feel that they are set aside, presenting a problem to the medical professionals as well as to the world. Their pregnancy becomes a very lonely place to be. Medical diagnosis is usually surrounded by negative language which speaks of how their child's body or mind has "something wrong" or how "a problem has been found". Suddenly, what was to be a joyful journey is marked by a negative narrative; it becomes a problematic and unexpected pathway that they must travel. The life of their child is judged to have less worth than that of children whose life follows a "normal" pattern of development. Parents are made to feel that they are adding something problematic to a harmonious world; the life of the child is not seen as gift; it is not felt to be good. The *BIA* approach challenges this negative starting point in a child's life and that of the child's parents. It does not accept the negative language that surrounds the pre-birth diagnosis. *BIA* invites you as an accompanier to focus on the knowledge that, within the creative activity of God, there is no norm for *being*, there is only a promise of belonging (Exodus 6:7), a knowledge that all life is good (Genesis 1:26-27) and teaching surrounding the richness of diversity (1 Corinthians 12:12-27). For however long a life lasts, in or out of the womb, all life is good in its diversity and all life is gift. This is the good news that we wish to share with parents. It is based on many years of attending to the stories, experience and requests of people who have been disabled and who have lived good and valued lives.

Before you move forward, take some time to reflect upon your personal and group approach to disability: what do you really think?

Scintilli of grace: *BIA* formation 2.1

Make a note of the immediate images or words that come into your mind when you see or hear the word:

Disability

Please reflect on the following and record your answer.

Notice how many of your words were negative and how many were positive.

The lives of some people, who are born within the goodness of God's rich diversity, have been disabled by negative attitudes, cultures, approaches and physical boundaries. If they have been born with a medical condition, with body shapes and ways of thinking that are not typical, their life is usually considered to be of less value than people who measure up to a typical way of being. Lack of access seems to follow them throughout their life because the world is mostly designed for a typically shaped body and way of processing information. As they seek to live their life in all its fullness (John 10:10) this lack of access restricts them from getting around or from using their creative skills to learn. They become disabled people. Some disabled people, in whose stories I have shared, have expressed how it felt knowing their life was a "disappointment", even before they were born. This has led them to live within a sense of loss, rather than experiencing their life as a gift.[8] I have always found this dismaying, for I have never met any person who is anything less than wonderful and whose hand is not held in God's. St John Paul II, himself a person who experienced being disabled, tells us how the human person is "unique and unrepeatable".[9] For St John Paul everybody "is capable of making visible what is invisible; the spiritual and divine".[10] Each body is "created to transfer into the visible reality of the world, the invisible mystery hidden in God, from time immemorial, and thus [is] a sign of it".[11] Here, St John Paul reveals that each person is a sign of God's mysterious love and presence in the world. God's grace is God's "loving communication with human existence",[12] it is how God touches our life.

Through the incarnation God becomes flesh, thus knowing and feeling what human existence entails. God desires to be with us and through Christ invites us into his company;[13] God wants to be in relationship with God's creation and to share in our lives. We know this through the scriptures, the teachings of the Christian Church, the actions and words of Christ, as his spirit moves throughout history among everyday people in their everyday lives (John 1:14-15). Jesus' human story leads us towards God; all our stories are part of this movement. We are orientated towards God's gaze and love; we turn towards God and God is always turned towards us. In moments that are challenging we might feel as if God is not present. However, these are moments when we are called to be held by God and be present with Christ (John 14:9-11). Recognising God's guidance in our human journeys, feeling the presence of Jesus, helps us to realise that in all things we are never alone; through uniting our lives with Christ's we are always held in God's love.[14] This is the essence of the Christian story. As I have travelled with families and individuals I have experienced how important it is to accompany people who find themselves on an unexpected path in their life and to support them as they "remain open to grace". In moments of extreme difficulty and grief, I have found that this has helped us to move forward. Reflecting on Christ's story helps us to realise that with every experience of the cross, there is always a resurrection.

Scintilli of grace: *BIA* formation 2.2

For personal or group reflection.

Think back into your own life. In difficult and joy-filled moments, how have you noticed God's presence at work in your life? How did God's touch reach into your life?

BIA formation 2.3

Reflections from the author and *BIA* parents

Parish accompaniment 2.3: insights

In my pastoral journeys, Psalm 139:1-18 has been a constant companion. The psalmists had a prophetic role in the Old Testament. As cantors and priests, their words and songs spoke for and to the people of God. Their poetic language served to express personal and collective experiences of spirituality, recording life's journey and mediating it to God. The psalms are therefore prayers from our ancestors in faith who have lived a life with God and whose words guide us and lead our own experiences and similar paths. Psalm 139 is a celebration of the human person and confirms that our God knows each one of us, just as we are. Each life has a purpose in God's plan; we each mirror God into the world. Throughout life, God and God's grace are our constant companions. God makes a profound yet simple promise for our existence: "I will be your God, and you shall be my people" (Jeremiah 7:23). We are therefore never alone and we *all*, *always* belong to God.

When a child and their parents receive a pre-birth diagnosis of a possible disability or medical condition, they find themselves in a situation that seems completely impossible. You can imagine them being very frightened of the huge responsibility that they are being asked to bear. My friend and colleague Dr Pia Matthews, herself a mother of a daughter with Rett syndrome,[15] tells us what she feels about the vocation of people with disabilities and gives an important message to parents:

> "People with disabilities can bring from within themselves exceptional energy and values of great use for the whole of humanity so that he or she is not only to whom we give; he or she must also be helped to become one who gives to the best of his or her ability."[16]

Pia helps us to see that becoming a parent is not just about having a child. Parents are called to enable each gift of life, for however long they live, to fulfil their personal call to vocation and experience their unique purpose in God's plan. Each person has a role in helping to teach the world what love is.

Receiving and giving life is not always straightforward. We can never know what is going to be asked of us. The gift of being a Christian is that we can be sure that, as we live, we are each held in God's gaze, and that it is this assurance that helps us to live faithfully, when life provides us with challenges that seem overwhelming. As Pia tells us, each life brings energy to the world, we are each given as God's gift to the world. No matter how long a child's life lasts, either in or out of the womb, or whatever medical diagnosis finds, a child will always be totally unique and unrepeatable; they are gift from the moment of their conception.

Some of the pathways that we travel are ones that we might have expected, and some take a different route. The birth of a child with a disability, the death of a child due to a medical condition, asks us to love. We are asked not to think of the child as a possession but as a person whose story we have been asked to nurture, to care for and to love. I have found that in the face of great suffering, choosing love as the driving force helps us spend time with an unborn child in a way that honours the child's story as well as the parents'. This does not, for any second, minimise the difficult path that they must follow, or the heart-wrenching experiences they will encounter. They will be facing issues of life and death and dealing with emotions that they had never thought to deal with. One of our parents shares his thoughts with us:

> "Everything seemed to be in slow motion, minute by minute and yet time passed so fast. From the scans we knew the physical challenges that our child would face, if he lived, so we knew what he had and through the scans we began to know who he was – a fighter. We thought about wheelchairs and the different

ways in which he would have to move, and our first thoughts were, can we do this, what sort of life will we have, what sort of life would he have? Speaking with my family helped me bring some perspective to his story. We placed love at the centre rather than fear. We began to see the wheelchair as the tool to enable him and that if we thought of his life as his life and not an extension of ours, new plans emerged, and we began to feel less frightened. Living in a wheelchair, or if he died in an operation would never change how much we loved him right now, as he grew in his own way."

Another family shared how they just could not decide what to do in the face of a life-threatening medical condition and how their visit to the priest helped them to keep focused on love:

"We talked with the priest. I thought that he would be the first to condemn us for considering a termination in such impossible circumstances but there was nothing like that. He did not tell us about suffering but recognised that there would be no painless option and that we needed to decide on the life of our child out of love for him and for ourselves. Thanks to our priest we met a person to accompany us with love. Thanks to their care for us, spiritual support and presence during the hard times, we are still together and trying to find God's love in all of this, trying to see the space for us in the Church."

Please read chapters 2 and 4 of the *BIA* parents' resource.

This is a time of intense formation for the *BIA* team. You can read individually or you may decide to invite one or two people to read and provide the team with a summarised presentation of the main insights. The information in each chapter will give you a full understanding of some of the issues and dilemmas that a child with a disability or medical condition faces as well as the challenges and hopes that parents may experience. The information and insights from this chapter will help you gain the "language of accompaniment" that you will need as you travel along the pathways with them. You will notice that:

1. The information and stories are written directly to the children and their parents.

2. Chapters 1, 3, 5 are often referred to during each chapter. These chapters are an imaginative remembering of the story of the unborn Christ child and the people who have been chosen to accompany his life and mission. The unique nature of this activity is that we have merged the experiences of the *BIA* parents with that of Christ's family by placing the words of the parents directly into the imaginative dialogue of Mary and Joseph. We gently recommend that you read these chapters if you would like to deepen your ability to accompany.

In this chapter we have met the experience of the unborn child and his or her parents as they face human, faith and moral dilemmas in their life. We have reflected upon the issues and mind-sets that they face in times of pre-birth diagnosis of a medical condition and possible experience of disability. We have invited you to meet and note your personal concept of disability as well as Christian teaching surrounding the dignity and value of life. We have suggested that Christian teaching assures a place of belonging for people who have been disabled by negative stereotypes and that within the promise of God and the body of Christ, everybody has a place. This chapter provides the base for the *BIA* approach and journey. It is the formation for the accompaniment you will give. We have highlighted how true Christian accompaniment is founded on love and not judgements or imposition of ideas and beliefs. We believe that through a witness to Christian teachings and love we are able to help families in challenging times.

Before you move forward please undertake the following activity.

Scintilli of grace: *BIA* insights and formation 2.4

For group discussion or individual reflection

Christian accompaniment requires us to bring a gentle energy into the life of others. It invites us to hold love of the neighbour at the centre of all we do.

Please discuss:

1. What has struck you the most from this chapter and that of the *BIA* parents' resource?

2. What are your main insights?

3. List the main issues you feel parents face.

4. How will you respond with love?

Bring all of your reflections into a time of prayer, where you will breathe with God and rest in God's company.

As we travel forward in the *BIA* journey, chapter 3 will invite you to spend some time becoming familiar with the *BIA* pathways that parents must follow. We will explain the main experiences that have been shared by *BIA* parents. You will be asked to read thought chapter 6 of the *BIA* parents' resource and become familiar with the advice that is shared.

CHAPTER THREE

EXPLAINING THE *BIA* PATHWAYS

The theological principle which underpins each of the *BIA* pathways proclaims that:

Each and every person is created in the image of God and as such is valued, loved and is an important member of the Church and the world.

This implicit principle is interwoven throughout the programme of formation and must be at the heart of your accompaniment. Before exploring how you can set up a *BIA* programme of formation in your parish, we would like to use this chapter to explain the pastoral context for the *BIA* journey. Chapter 3 will share some of the experiences that parents have shared concerning their journeys and will show how the MEET process can work on differing levels and at different stages.

The pastoral context: the *BIA* journey

The individual encounter: the journey begins

In our previous chapters and throughout the *BIA* parents' resource, we explain how the parents are on a very delicate journey with their child in the womb. Usually their starting point, in the *BIA* journey, begins with the first scan when the child is identified as having a disability. It is, usually, at this point that the parents' need for support begins. We recommend that a parish undertakes all of the three *BIA* stages, so that they might be ready to accompany any family who find themselves on such a pathway.

Exploring the *BIA* pathways

We will now explore the four different *BIA* pathways which parents may experience once they receive the news that their unborn child has a medical diagnosis concerning disability. It is important to remember that for each pathway the parents face an unexpected journey. Maintaining and affirming the value, dignity and full humanity of their child, along with the love that the parish has for the family, will accompany them on their journey. In a time when many negative voices and opinions may surround them, the accompaniment of a parish team can provide a positive and loving alternative space to that of the many appointments and, in the words of one of the *BIA* parents, "mountain of medical terminology, which quickly become part of [their] life". In such difficult times, the words of Pope Francis should be at the heart of the way in which you accompany; in all times of great pastoral need, the answer is love: not the false kind but one that is "true, concrete and respectful".[17] Such concrete love will support the family, so that they can know that they are loved and not alone as they travel forward. Having set up your parish team you will now be invited to explore the issues that parents may face as well as the advice that we have provided for them in the *BIA* parents' book. Please now read through the summaries below and follow directives concerning the parents' resource.

The four *BIA* pathways:

BIA Pathway 1

Receiving the news that the child has a medical condition and that they could experience being disabled. The parents choose to continue with the pregnancy but the baby does not reach term and his or her life ends naturally in the womb.

BIA Pathway 2

Receiving the news that the child has a medical condition and could die soon after birth. The parents choose to continue with the pregnancy and prepare for palliative care post-birth.

BIA Pathway 3

Receiving the news that the child has a medical condition and that the mother's life may be at risk. Having exhausted all possibilities, the parents feel that they have no other option than termination.

BIA Pathway 4

Receiving the news that the baby will be born either at term or prematurely and that the child may experience being disabled in his or her life. This may be explained as the child "having a disability". The parents continue with the pregnancy. The baby is born with a possible experience of disability, lives and goes home with parents.

Scintilli of grace: *BIA* formation 3.1: exploring the *BIA* pathways and advice

Please read through the summaries below. When you have done this please read through the general advice that is found in chapter 6 of the *BIA* parents' resource. Each road records a different pastoral situation that will ask for differing responses and empathy as they are accompanied.

You may like to do this individually or you may choose to do this as a team. You could ask four people to explore one pathway each. They could then summarise their learning and deliver it to the group. You should all become familiar with the pastoral context of each pathway.

Explaining the *BIA* pathways: summarised

Each pathway is colour-coded in the *BIA* parents' resource. The parents are guided to choose the pathway that best explores their particular experience. Each summary below presents three perspectives: the child's, which always comes first, the parents' and the accompaniers'.

Pathway 1

The child's perspective

At all times, the life of the child should be acknowledged for who the child is and not the medical condition that the child has been diagnosed as having. The child should be recognised as an individual. In line with personal and religious beliefs, the parents choose to travel with their child as far to term as is possible. Where there are siblings, their needs should also be included in the support you provide. You must always negotiate, with parents, the best way to help children cope with the pastoral situation and the life of their brother or sister.

The parents' perspective

The parents receive the news that their child has a medical condition and could experience being disabled. Following consultation with doctors they receive advice regarding the life of their unborn child and her or his eventual medical condition. Following this and further tests the parents are invited to discuss the eventual options that are available to them from the health service. The family's faith perspective should be acknowledged, respected and included in their medical and spiritual care. It should be clear that mother and baby are seen as two patients with individual, medical and emotional needs. In Pathway 1, the parents decide to continue with the pregnancy as far as possible. The baby's medical condition may be such that she or he does not reach term and his or her life ends naturally in the womb.

Parish accompaniment: issues to consider

It is important to help parents who travel this pathway to know that they have done all that they can to nurture and respect the life of their child. They have loved their child into being and have nurtured the baby for the whole of her or his life. Everything that they have done has been out of love. They have found themselves in a moral and spiritual dilemma, for which they may not have been prepared. On this pathway they will experience loss, grief and will need time to mourn. The parish should accompany them through this time using the *BIA* approach. The *BIA* accompaniment must continue for the months and years that follow birth and beyond. The parents and their child have a very important place in the Church. This is the same for the whole family. The parents are a witness to love. Remembering the baby, within the parish community, is a vital part of the healing process on this pathway and we would encourage you to mark the baby's life within an experience of parish/private worship/prayer (according to wishes of parents). The *BIA* parish team should work with the parish priest/pastor to create a memorial liturgy following the baby's delivery. This should be commemorated each year after the baby has died.

Pathway 2

The child's perspective

At all times, the life of the child should be acknowledged for who the child is and not the medical condition that the child has been diagnosed as having. The child should be recognised as an individual. In line with personal and religious beliefs, the parents choose to travel with their child as far to term as is possible. Where there are siblings, their needs should also be included in the support you provide. You must always negotiate, with parents, the best way to help children cope with the pastoral situation and the life of their brother or sister.

The parents' perspective

The parents receive the news that their child has a medical condition and could experience being disabled. The parents consider the medical condition that has been diagnosed and take advice from the doctors, regarding the life of their unborn child. Following this and further tests, the parents are invited to discuss the eventual options that are available to them from their health service. However, the news is that the medical condition is such that the baby may die, very soon after birth. They decide that they wish to carry the baby to term or as far as is possible. The choice has been to select palliative care post-birth. The parents must always know that they have loved their child for the whole of his or her life.

Parish accompaniment: issues to consider

It is important to help parents who travel this pathway to know that they have done all that they can to nurture and respect the life of their child. They have loved their child into being and have nurtured the baby for the whole of her or his life. Everything that they have done has been out of love. They have found themselves in a moral and spiritual dilemma, for which they may not have been prepared. On this pathway they will experience loss, grief and will need time to mourn. The parish should accompany them through this time using the *BIA* approach. The *BIA* accompaniment must continue for the months and years that follow birth and beyond. The parents and their child have a very important place in the Church. This is the same for the whole family. The parents are a witness to love. Remembering the baby, within the parish community, is a vital part of the healing process on this pathway and we would encourage you to mark the baby's life within an experience of parish/private worship/prayer (according to wishes of parents). The *BIA* parish team should work with the parish priest/pastor to create a memorial liturgy following the baby's delivery. This should be commemorated each year after the baby has died.

Pathway 3

A note from the author

I have found this to be the most delicate and difficult pathway for parents to travel. Parents may find themselves under unbelievable pressure to choose termination as a "solution" to expecting a child with a medical diagnosis. However, Christian teaching takes seriously its protection of all human life and can never advocate termination as an option to a medical diagnosis. Parents may be subject to a lack of pastoral services and feel that their options have been exhausted, choosing reluctantly to travel this path. The *BIA* programme seeks to accompany parents as they travel through such dilemmas. They may have arrived at this point against their will or religious beliefs.

The child's perspective

At all times, the life of the child should be acknowledged for who the child is and not the medical condition that the child has been diagnosed as having. The child should be recognised as an individual. The child's life will end at termination. Where there are siblings, their needs should also be included in the support you provide. As this is such a difficult issue you must always negotiate, with parents, the best way to help children cope with the pastoral situation and the life of their brother or sister.

The parents' perspective

On this pathway the parents find themselves in extreme spiritual and moral dilemmas. Having exhausted all possibilities and often under possible external pressure, they may consider following medical guidance to terminate during the pregnancy. Parents may have faced difficulty in having their religious or spiritual needs considered or understood during consultations. Parents may be feeling overwhelmed by all of the medical information that they must deal with. While this is not the road that Christian parents would wish to travel, they often have to face the prospect of termination. This road is, however, final and arrives at an assurance of death. It is important to remember that at the end of this pathway parents may have difficulty with experiencing closure. They may also take on huge amounts of guilt as the final outcome has been something that they have chosen to do. Parents must never be judged for this and must always know that they have loved their child for the whole of his or her life.

Parish accompaniment: issues to consider

In chapter 6 of the *BIA* parents' resource we provide important perspectives from Christian teaching. We would ask you to become familiar with this information so that you are able to share the information with parents as they need it. We hope this will help you identify what the Christian Church teaches and what

other options parents may be able to ask the hospital to consider, before deciding that this pathway is the one that they will take. This pathway, while not supported by church teachings, calls for honest, pastoral and loving accompaniment that is non-judgemental, recognising the agonising decisions that parents are faced with. It is this that *BIA* seeks to provide. You should not advise parents but aim to always be a listening, supporting and prayerful presence. If it is impossible for them to make a decision, or as they make the decision, you should help them look for professional help.

A *BIA* parent shared that: "We went for therapy with a person that works with parents like us. She was very honest, quite scary sometimes, but she helped us a lot. She was not afraid to challenge us, to ask us questions we did not want to hear, and to hear our own thoughts."

Pathway 4

The child's perspective

On this pathway the child is diagnosed with a possible experience of disability. The baby, as with all babies, is unique, loved and created by God. He or she is a perfect gift from God. In the eyes of God and of all God's people, the child's life can never be held within any idea of being a "shame". In the child's own unique way and for the time that is his or hers to live, the child will image God, they will reflect God (Genesis 1:26-27). "The image of God is not a quality that we earn but reflects the loving relationship that our loving creator maintains with each one of us."[18] The birth of this child begins a creative and hope-filled journey. This will be accompanied by the richness of diversity. It will be a colourful life. You can read more about this approach to the life of disabled people in the "Living Fully Statement" (appendix of this resource).

The parents' perspective

On this pathway you should encourage the parents to recognise the arrival of their child as gift. The *BIA* approach to the child's life is one that seeks to enable the gift of life. *BIA* invites parents to shift from the negative language that might surround their child's life. Applying this positive approach rejects seeing their child as "having something wrong" with him or her, but notices the potential in the child's life. Their child is an image of God and is called to a personal vocation with Christ. The child has a vital place within the body of Christ, and without his or her witness and love the body of Christ is incomplete (1 Corinthians 12:12-27).

44

Parish accompaniment: issues to consider

Holding a positive attitude towards the child's life and needs will enable the parents to feel that they can approach the child's life with hope. Your approach must be enabling not disabling. The baby and his or her family must be assured of the love of the Christian community and the rights that they have to enjoy all that the Church provides. The baby will be an important witness to the gift of life and love. The Christian community must always be grateful for the wonder of life and all that the family has contributed to the body of Christ and their reflection of the *imago Dei*. If the baby has been baptised under a state of emergency you will also have to work with the parents to help organise a parish liturgy of welcome. The parish should be advised of the liturgy and be part of the celebration where possible or where agreed. In this way the parents are able to see and feel all that is possible for their child as they bring energy to the parish and prepare for their own life with grace

BIA formation 3.2:
reflections from the author and *BIA* parents

Parish accompaniment: insight

Over the past twenty-five years I have spent most of my time studying God, but it was not until I received the news of my grandson's pre-birth diagnosis that I was challenged to move from knowledge about Christian love to an embodied experience of accompaniment. When my son and daughter-in-law had received the news of Giorgio's disability, they mentioned how hard it was to have to keep telling people "over and over again what was wrong". It just made them feel more helpless. My son told me that "when people gave their opinions, it was difficult to listen to". Here, as a theologian, all my words fell into a new place. I realised that it was not for me to teach them about the dignity of life but to accompany through love and understanding. My son confirmed that it was much more helpful when people just sat and listened and told him "that it was OK to cry", or when people realised that they just needed a break, or a place to be and spend time with their unborn child.

As Christians we are called to be accompaniers. In 2013 I was privileged to work alongside the International Association of Catholic Bioethicists, who met to explore how the life of the unborn child and his or her parents could be supported by the Church. Our final statement suggests that: "Suffering always calls for solidarity by Christians with those who suffer and mourn. And that Christian solidarity is manifested through sincere gift of 'oneself' by showing heartfelt concern, being with those who suffer and mourn, and providing love, loving care and support."[19]

Christian accompaniment does not entail making judgements about people's decisions or telling them what to do. It is about being with them as they travel through the teachings and insights of their faith tradition and supporting their life in a way that helps them to know they are not alone. One of our *BIA* mothers told me:

> "I felt unable to make a decision. I wanted somebody as knowledgeable as God to come and tell me all the details, the future, what I should do. I looked for his voice everywhere, in the Church, charity organisations, friends, doctors, parents but nothing really helped me to feel I am doing the right things. My strongest emotions were dread, rage and that God has forsaken me. I did not like it when people told me that 'I do not know what I would do in your situation' because what it meant was 'You are on your own.' I did meet some wonderful people during this time and rediscovered my sister; all of them helped me to deal with the situation in different ways. I much preferred it when people would actually spend their time to think about it with me."

As Pope Francis told priests and the world, at the Chrism Mass on Maundy Thursday 2018, "Closeness involves an attitude that engages the whole person, our way of relating, our way of being attentive to both ourselves and others." These words add to one of the most important features of the *BIA* approach, whereby we do not seek to provide parents with a decision or a solution, but to accompany them with the insights and wisdom of families and thinkers, who have lived and travelled with God. Accompaniment matters because their story matters. As Pope Francis tells us, "Like the Holy Family of Nazareth, every family is part of the history of people; it cannot exist without the generations who have gone before it."[20]

Below you will find the basic principles of Christian accompaniment. After you have read these we will invite you to pray, individually or as a team, inviting God's grace to accompany you as you prepare to accompany parents with love.

Active listening: some basic guidelines[21]

The following guidelines will help you receive the story of parents. We hope that it will help parents share their story. You can use them alongside the *BIA* approach and invite people to encounter *BIA* principles when sharing time with you. You will also be able to use them to help you when you spend time with parents, professionals, chaplains and fellow parishioners.

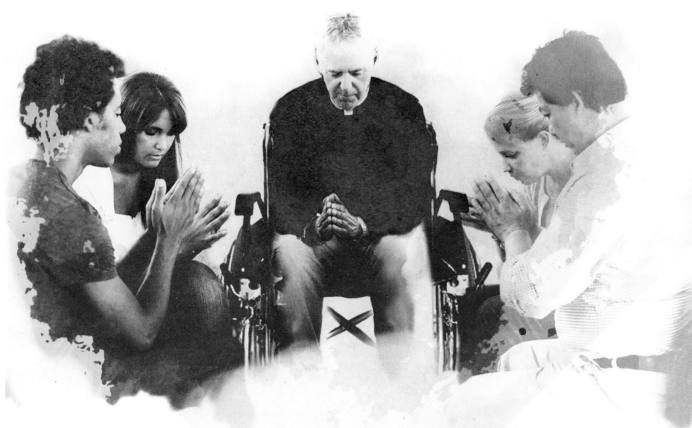

Active listening requires respect for every person's story; this will include the life and potential of the unborn child.

Confidentiality is the most important practice of any one or any team of accompaniers. Parents must feel safe to share their story, knowing it will not be repeated or laid open for judgement. Anything that is said must be kept confidential.

Accompaniers should not project opinions but receive stories with love.

Active listening cannot be rushed. It requires the gift of time and a suitable environment that can provide privacy and a safe space to express emotions. You will need time and space so that you can *be with* parents and their unborn child, helping them to think and notice what they feel.

In the same way that Jesus met and shared in people's story, so must we. Accompanying people with love asks you to recognise that you are on sacred ground when in the presence of their experience. Please don't share opinions but accompany parents in a way that is right for them.

An active listener helps parents look to the future in the light of choices that are made. You must not bulldoze parents into making decisions based on your own convictions but give gentle witness to the *BIA* approach and Christian teaching on the gift of life.

Negative comments about lack of faith, healing and punishment for sins in the light of their pre-birth diagnosis are not compatible with Christian teaching on the life of each human being. Parents must not be subjected to such mistaken concepts. If you notice such behaviour please put an end to it pastorally but immediately.

People act in different ways when they hear the news of a pre-birth diagnosis and might be very insensitive during the parents' decision-making process. One parent told us about their experience and provides parents with some advice about what they can do in such situations: "They might push you to think like them, take for granted that you will make certain decisions, which is very ignorant. Do not try to fight them or convince them; try to help them understand your point of view. If it is very hard for you to listen to what they say, you may to want to ask them not to contact you, even if it is somebody very close to you, like a parent or sibling."

When you are sharing, help parents to feel confident in defining what they are feeling and be sure to create an environment whereby they feel safe to share what is in their heart. Your accompaniment matters more than advice in difficult times.

Active listening involves taking the parents' and child's story seriously and wanting to share in a family's journey. Getting to know their story and needs will enable you to be with them when they need you.

All accompaniers in your team must work from the *BIA* approach and theological standpoint, as stated at the start of this chapter. Please note that what people feel is important and what they feel about the future.

As accompaniers you should assure parents of your desire to be with them. Please take time to help them look for information that will help them on their journey. Your support should be based upon Christian love. The family, whatever the outcome of the diagnosis, will hold an important place of belonging within the church and community. Please be sure to affirm this throughout the parents' journey.

Work with parents to develop a pastoral plan that can be activated surrounding birth or in times of loss. Together, form a process that parents can activate during important moments, which can include: after scans, hospital appointments, meetings with consultant, birth and more especially during times surrounding birth and death. You must be guided by the parents and times for accompaniment must be as agreed.

Developing a pastoral plan with parents: important information
(this can also be found in chapter 6 of the *BIA* parents' resource)

Baptism at the start and end of life

Baptism by desire can be administered by a pastor. Christian teaching (mainly Lutheran, the Anglican Communion and Roman Catholic Church) explains that those who desire baptism, but are not baptised with water through the Christian sacrament (because of death), can nevertheless receive the fruits of baptism at the moment of death. Parents may ask for their child to receive a baptism by desire, stating their desire for the life of their child.

The *Catechism of the Catholic Church* (1259) states that "For catechumens who die before their Baptism, their [or their parents' – author's addition] explicit desire to receive it, together with repentance for their sins, and charity, assures them the salvation that they were not able to receive through the sacrament."

What you might need to know about baptism under a state of emergency

Baptism is the initiation into the life of Christ and the Christian community. It would usually be administered in a church by a minister. Parents are asked to bring their child to baptism soon after the child's birth, thus sharing their faith and accompanying the life of their child with faith. Where a baby is in danger of death, soon after birth, a lay person can conduct a baptism under a state of emergency. This should only happen in the absence of a chaplain or pastor. An example of this is found in the rite of baptism of the Catholic Church, which states that when a person is in danger of imminent death: "any member of the faithful, indeed anyone with the right intention, may and sometimes must administer baptism" (*Christian Initiation, General Introduction*, 16).

You should organise a meeting with parents and their pastor (or the hospital chaplain) so that they are aware of the parents' pastoral need and choices. Together you could write a plan for any eventual emergency. This is so that you will be prepared and be able to bring comfort to the family by the prayer that you have created together. Please include siblings in the plan so that they may have a role in the baby's life. Each Christian tradition uses different rites and rituals but generally for emergency baptisms:

1. You should have a witness if possible; the midwife may be happy to do this.

2. You should use sterile water, especially if the baby needs emergency surgery.

3. The person who baptises should pour water three times over the baby's head where possible. If not, they should dip their hand in the water and place it on the baby's head.

4. The person who baptises should say the baby's name, followed by, "I baptise you in the name of the Father [pour water], and of the Son [pour water], and of the Holy Spirit [pour water]."

In the joyful case of the child not dying, the parish community should plan and share a welcome liturgy for the baby, and for the family. In the sadness of a child dying, you should follow up with a memorial service, or help the family to plan a funeral.

Handing the child to God

In the sadness of the baby dying in the womb, during birth or immediately after birth, we suggest that the family conduct a handover prayer time. This can be shared with a pastor, chaplain, family or whomever the family wish to share with. This can take place as soon as they know that the baby has died or just before the parents know that the baby will be delivered.

You might help parents to plan as follows:

1. Play some gentle music; it may be music that parents have shared with their unborn child during their pregnancy.

2. Place a cross on a table and invite parents to share memories from their time with their child in the womb.

3. Words that can be used: "Father, you breathed _____ [child's name] into being. We/I thank you for _____'s time in our lives. We have shared love with _____ and now hand _____ back to you. Lord, Father, Son and Spirit, may he/she rest with you in peace."

4. Invite parents to spend some time with God, in silence, in tears. This is time to be with God as God welcomes their child home.

5. Read the words below:

   - WITH YOU, O LORD, ALL IS MADE POSSIBLE…
     MAY WE FEEL YOUR PRESENCE IN OUR SADNESS.

   - "IN OUR TIME OF GREAT SADNESS AND SEPARATION WE STAY IN YOUR PRESENCE. YOU HELD US BY YOUR HAND, NOW GUIDE ME"
     (BASED ON PSALM 73:23).

Travelling through grief, with grace

Grief is never easy to travel through. It is one of the most challenging of all human emotions. However, to grieve means to have loved; we know that we have loved when we miss the person we grieve for. The most fundamental need for any human being is to be loved; this is the deepest call from the life of the unborn child. For parents to grieve for the child that is lost is to cry out from the experience of the child being present; because the child has been  present, they have been called to love. When the child is absent, the heart is at a loss. Grieving, crying, showing sadness, expressing the emptiness that they are feeling, is an important part of the healing process. Grief is the process of psychological, behavioural, social and physical reactions to loss. It is a continuing process involving many changes over time.[22] It is a natural reaction to loss and death. Mourning is a way of expressing emotions and resolving feelings of grief. Grief is different for each person, and no one person grieves in the same way as others. It is important to give people space and time to come to terms with loss. While you can provide some advice about managing grief, you should also explore where parents might access counselling services. We recommend this for a whole family, especially if the unborn child has siblings. Parish accompaniment should help the parents find a service that will take their faith and beliefs into serious consideration.

Accompaniers should respect the experiences of grief they will encounter. Be with parents as they live though grief, gently encouraging parents to keep their gaze on Christ, who travelled though death so that we "might share in his resurrection",[23] there is always hope where there is love.

BIA formation 3.3:
reflections from the author and *BIA* parents

Attending to experience

In any situation that involves suffering, pastoral responses tend to use language that links our suffering to that of Christ. This can be a very difficult concept to accept when we are living though a painful situation. While it is true that our lives are linked to Christ's sufferings, for he was born, died and rose so that we might know God, many of our parents, in the words of one of them, were not able to "hear that I shared in Christ's suffering, I preferred not to!" In an interesting book, *Beauty and Brokenness*,[24] Martin Lloyd Williams, the author, a parent of a young man with Down syndrome, suggests that "we must not go down the offensive way of thinking that suffering is beautiful if it brings us closer to God, suffering is never beautiful".[25] Suffering, I feel, is part of the rise and fall of life, it is something that we all experience at certain times in our life. In my work with parents I have learned from their resilience and ability to move through times of deep anguish and suffering with grace.

I have witnessed many stories of great love and commitment, where parents have accepted the "depths of one's humanity, the depths of life".[26] I feel that suffering is not a way of being drawn closer to God, as if we need to suffer to know God; I believe that God is already close to us in our suffering. God is right there with us and knows what it is like, God's story is evidence of this, confirmed by one of our *BIA* parents as she shared about her own experience of losing her unborn child.

"I did not feel God's grace, but I also don't feel his punishment. I think God is simply crying together with the parents when they are losing their baby."

In chapters 1, 3 and 5 of the *BIA* parents' resource we took parents on an imaginative journey through the life story of Jesus with Mary and Joseph. We entered into the reality and depths of Christ's unborn life. We remembered his conception, his experience of rejection, his safety in the womb and his being born to suffer, with the sure knowledge of his resurrection, the redemption promised as he was presented in the Temple (Luke 2:22-28). We noted his parents' worries about him being rejected, their joys and disappointments, their need for companionship and support. These are all the lived experiences that I have shared with parents who travel similar pathways in life to the ones that the parents you accompany may be on.

In our imaginative journey into the Christian traditions that underpin our faith, we noted how God remained with them, constantly reminding them along their pathway to keep focused on God, that God is always close. Suffering is not beautiful, but it is most definitely something that people should not experience alone; it is a joint path on which we must suffer the rises and the falls together. I have also learnt how some parents have been traumatised at the hands of some negative encounters with zealous Christians who have insisted that they should pray for forgiveness and ask God for a cure for their child. This incorrect understanding of disability serves only to suggest that some people are less perfect than others. A child with an experience of disability does not need to be cured, for, as we have seen in our reflections thus far, the child is already perfect and already loved. The parents, their child and their family are perfect gifts from God, just as they are and "because they are".

For Christians, each of life's experiences is a call to know and live with God in the assurance of God's promise: "I will be your God and you will be my people, we belong together."[27] The experience of suffering must not be added to by experiences of abandonment. Parents must be supported by a positive and fully Christian love that celebrates the life of the unborn child. This Christian approach is at the heart of the *BIA* journey and must be part of the witness that you give to love as you accompany.

One of our *BIA* parents found the book *The Shaming of the Strong*[28] very helpful. In this book, the Williams family provide a testimony and gentle learning. The book tells of a love story between a family and their unborn daughter and sibling, whom they know physically for just a brief time but whose spirit and witness, would be with them for ever. The story shares how they were able to move through suffering so as to nurture her unborn presence. The family's belief in God's call to love gave them the confidence to search for grace and look to the future. Sarah Williams tells us very movingly how she began to understand the Trinity more through her suffering and the love she felt for her daughter. Very powerfully she bears witness to how this experience in her and her family's life was about self-giving. She, very beautifully, explains how she may not be able to share her love with her child in a way that she would wish to but that this could never remove the love that she had shared, that they had all shared, from her daughter's conception to her death. This is a very important message for parents who travel similar roads, whether their child is born and lives with an experience of disability or whether the child's medical condition calls him or her to be reunited with God, the Father, the Son and the Spirit. We are asked to be "in love" for the whole of our lives.

Let us now spend some time with some more stories from our *BIA* parents, who express how they were able to travel though suffering and show how important it is to be accompanied with love and not judgement.

"Our son was born so fast. We knew of his disabilities and as he was born we were just amazed by him. He was taken away and put into intensive care and we were told that he needed a life-saving operation. We had already decided to baptise him and so gave him baptism under a state of emergency so that we all might know God's strength, love and accompaniment. Gently, accompanied by the midwives and each other, we handed our son to God though baptism, knowing he would be accompanied no matter what happened. They were harrowing hours but we knew that God was with us, we just knew."

"As with all things in our life journeys, we learn to live in the moment and adapt to our situations, seeking for something to pull us through to the future, to what the future may be like with our son's physical abilities and needs. I wish I could go back in time, knowing what I know now and how the hardship and worry, the pain, is only temporary, in amongst the real happiness and joy of loving your child just as they are."

"We met some people in the church who were terrifying, speaking of brain transplants and God's judgement for people like us. The only good stories, we were told, were about situations where people were praying for miracles and where parents were rewarded with a child who only had a slight disability. We found this dangerous and were steered away from this by people who could give alternative perspectives; there was never any prejudice, and it helps reassure me that God loves us no matter what our predicament."

"Some of the worst moments of suffering came when I went to church from people who pushed their understanding of healing onto us. Their implication that we weren't being faithful enough by not praying for our daughter to be healed and live was very painful. I'd felt God had spoken very clearly over our daughter's diagnosis and felt she would receive the ultimate healing of going to be with Jesus, but some people tried to push us to have more faith (which I had plenty of, thank you very much!)."

"My husband's experience has been quite different. His experience of God has been one of feeling anger and rage, followed by a loss of faith. The consultant had planned a birth to allow spontaneous delivery as much as possible, to create as little stress as possible for her fragile body. As soon as she was out the midwives placed her straight onto my chest for skin to skin. My husband and I kissed and talked to her as she quietly passed away. One of the midwives came back at the end of her shift and after saying goodbye to me, leaned down to our baby's cold cot and kissed her goodbye on the forehead. That meant more to me than I could ever hope to express as it made the statement that my daughter not only mattered but was loved by more than just ourselves."

"Both our old and our new officers from our Salvation Army community, along with various teams at the corps, helped us to plan a beautiful funeral for our daughter… we received great pastoral care."

"Straight after delivery I was strangely calm, even happy that I could meet my baby, even though he was dead. I wanted to hug him and touch him, but at the same time I could see that all of this was damaging his very delicate skin, that his body was decomposing. It was really heartbreaking to see it. His cremation brought us back to the origin. The service was difficult, but it was also beautiful and human. We received lots of kindness and understanding from everybody involved. It was a very small service, with the people who were very close and dear to us. We felt that nobody but the four of us ever cared for him, ever knew him enough to be invited."

Scintilli of grace: *BIA* formation 3.4: an individual or parish team activity

Please reread all of the stories from the *BIA* parents. If you work as a team, take it in turns to read one of the stories aloud. As they are read out, the rest of the team should practise active listening.

Following this discuss:

- What strikes you about the stories from the *BIA* parents?

- What difficulties can you identify?

- Where can you find God's presence?

In this chapter we have explained four different pathways that parents will follow. We have encouraged you to read through chapter 6 of the *BIA* parents' resource for a more in-depth understanding. We have wanted to explain some of the most important issues that we feel you will face and provide you with tools and methods for engaging in Christian accompaniment. In chapter 4 we will explore how to run a *BIA* journey in your parish. Before we travel forward, we now invite you to pray.

As a parish team or individually:

Take time now to breathe with God, to pray. Allow yourself to feel God's presence. Invite Father, Son and Spirit to lead you as you prepare to accompany parents on their journeys. Reflect on how you will live out God's call to accompany and write down what you feel God guides you towards.

As a group or alone, remain ever present and aware of the moments of grace that you can share with parents as they stay present to God. Share with each other and allow this prayer time to form your practice of accompaniment.

We assure you of our love;

you are not alone;

let us pray.

CHAPTER FOUR

THE *BIA* PROGRAMME OF FORMATION

Exploring and accompanying the story

As you have discovered from our journey together thus far, you may meet parents as they travel along any of the four pathways we have explained in chapter 3. The *BIA* pathways are not representative of all experiences that parents might encounter but summarise the pastoral contexts for which most parents need accompaniment. Chapter 4 will invite you to explore how you can bring all of the learning you have undertaken into parish ministry. Wherever possible, you should be ready to support parents. The *BIA* programme will help you to:

- be proactive in setting up a *BIA* programme of Christian accompaniment in your parish;

- ensure that you have services ready if an urgent need arises;

- respond positively, should any person be in need at any point of their personal journey;

- make an immediate response if the pastoral needs should arise without any warning.

You may have decided to run a *BIA* journey following the lack of support for a family you know. You may be a parent who has travelled a similar path in the absence of accompaniment. You may be a parish team who have decided that you would like to provide support for families who receive a pre-birth diagnosis or you may have decided to undertake the *BIA* journey due to a family being in urgent need of support and accompaniment. For whatever reason you are using this resource, we hope the *BIA* programme will allow you to accompany unborn children and their parents in a way that is immediate and authentic.

Aims and objectives of the *BIA* programme of formation

- Provide support for parents who receive a pre-birth diagnosis of a medical condition for their child.

- Enable the parents to know their place of belonging.

- Support parents emotionally, practically and spiritually as they receive news of their child's needs and the pathways they will travel with their unborn child.

- Ensure that parents do not feel alone.

- Develop a parish programme of accompaniment; develop a parish team of accompaniers.

- Increase disability awareness in the parish/service so as to remove barriers that disabled people face.

- Develop chaplaincy services and ensure pastoral support for parents experiencing trauma in pregnancy.

- Live out the Christian theology of the gift of life.

- Spend time with each other, sharing in stories and cooperating with grace.

- Live as the Church, the people of God, acting, praying and accompanying each other with love.

Where do we start ?

We have designed the journey to have three separate starting points. This is so that you can choose the journey that best suits your pastoral needs. You can choose:

- **BIA start-point 1:** to help you raise awareness and build a ministry in your parish or chaplaincy service;

- **BIA start-point 2:** to help you set up a programme of formation for Christian accompaniment so that you may be ready if the needs arise;

- **BIA start-point 3:** to develop an Immediate Response Strategy (IRS) to an urgent request for accompaniment.

You can choose which start-point meets your most urgent need. It is important that, if the need arises, a family has someone to turn to who can provide an alternative experience to the negativity they may encounter following a pre-birth diagnosis. Each start-point sets forth a programme of formation, using the MEET method. This will help you to remember complex information and respond quickly if you need to. Following this, chapter 5 will provide you with a final reflection on the BIA journey to encourage you to use the information from the BIA resources to set up a ministry in your parish.

The *BIA* journey explained

MEET, a portable tool for your programme of accompaniment

M: Meet

Parents have already spent time with their child in the womb. They go to the scan appointment with certain expectations and receive a diagnosis that their child has a medical condition and that they may experience a possible disability. The parents usually experience an immediate sense of anxiety. It is also a graced moment where the family meet an image of their child in the womb. The parents will meet the medical condition that their child is identified as having and may meet a series of new doctors and specialists. They may also meet negative attitudes and language surrounding the life of the child. It is important to know this information about their life but it does not identify who the child is or reflect the gift that the child brings to the world and the Church.

E: Explain

The doctors begin to explain the medical needs of the child. This is usually done from within a medical model of disability where it is seen that the child has a deficit due to a medical condition. More often than not the family is told that there is "something wrong" with the child in the womb rather than explaining what potential or gifts the child might hold. Parents often name this as the most difficult part of the journey. Please remember that this is a life-changing moment. You will generally meet parents following such an event as this is when they may turn to a pastor/priest for help. It is not time to offer advice, to make judgements or to tell people what to do. Here you must offer a safe space for their story to be held in love and a promise of accompaniment. The parents must feel they are not alone. If the unborn child has siblings, their accompaniment will also need to be planned for.

E: Explore – this is where the pastoral team must be at its most active.

During this time, the family begin to undergo many medical explorations and tests which seek to identify the medical condition of the child. The body of the baby becomes a place for tests rather than a place of wonder and the mother's womb becomes a place for anxiety rather than a creative space for grace. The child's life is usually assigned to a deficit model within the human story and is surrounded by negative language. During this time parents have to dig deep to explore their emotions and how they might notice *scintilli*: they are often "surrounded by language of termination with some evidence of there being an expectation that ending the child's life is the most responsible answer to the problem they have found". This was a common experience of the *BIA* parents. During this time parents will need heightened but sensitive accompaniment.

The support you give *must not* be judgemental as parents are facing unexpected and moral dilemmas. They have to deal with issues that lie at the very foundation of life and consider how they might cooperate with God's call and with their religious beliefs. Tests will continue, medical news may continue to be given in a way that is "more negative and frightening each time" they attend the hospital. Family and friends may respond negatively or sympathetically and parents may feel pitied instead of blessed. During this time, it is important that the family feel that their child is a life to be celebrated and that their story is important. They must know that they are being held in the love of the pastoral team and in the prayers of the parish (you can find guidance in chapter 6 of the *BIA* parents' resource for each pathway).

Exploring how to accompany

Meeting with other parents who have travelled this journey will help the family to explore in a way that is empathic. The *BIA* team must be an alternative voice of acceptance and should help the family to experience belonging. The *BIA* team will help the family explore the possibilities that their gift of life holds with them, in the Church and the world. It is very important that the parish is a welcoming community. The attention given to issues of disability within the everyday life of the parish is a witness to an *authentic* culture of belonging which is borne out in practice. Positive language will help the family act with love and guide them to reflect upon the fact that they will "love their child for the whole of their life".[29] Your positive accompaniment will help parents cooperate with God's call in their life, rather than think about their child as "not being what they had wanted or expected". Time for prayer and contemplation will be an important part of the team's action at this time. Accompaniers should undertake both personal and collective prayer. Praying with the parents and the child will be important.

T: Transcend

The parents continue to discern their future lives, accompanied by the pastoral teams and the *BIA* approach; the family will be questioning what life will be like with a disabled child, what help they might have and also whom they will be able to turn to. Some parents will be facing the certain death of their child and will be preparing to travel through grief. During this time, parents are faced with serious choices and decisions; it is a time of confusion and ongoing anxiety. Time for prayer and contemplation will be an important part of the action of the team and experience of the parents. *BIA* teams will continue to travel with parents during this time. They will help plan for liturgies and prayer times before, through and after birth. *BIA* teams will share in regular meetings with parents and will help plan for liturgies of welcome, baptism by desire, handover prayer and baptism under a state of emergency, as well as the funeral if the child does not live. The role of the *BIA* team is to look to the future with hope, while ministering in the present with love. You should accompany the parents to know that, when travelling through an experience of the cross, there is always the knowledge of the resurrection.

Running a *BIA* journey in your parish

MEET in three "start-points"

Start-point 1 (SP1): Parish/chaplaincy organisation level

This start-point aims to raise the awareness of theology and disability in your service. It will help you review practices and plan to make changes if needs be. This stage should be activated before you begin to form parish accompaniers. It should begin as soon as you have finished exploring the *BIA* resources. If your parish has already undergone a programme of disability awareness, and you wish to apply the *BIA* approach, you could proceed directly to SP2. However, it is always recommended to revisit your services as set out in stage 1. *This stage is aimed at facilitating parish/service development.*

Start-point 2 (SP2): The *BIA* programme of formation

This start-point aims to set out the *BIA* programme of formation. SP2 should begin as soon as you have finalised the activities identified in SP1. It can also be activated prior to a pastoral need arising or if an IRS should be needed suddenly. *This stage is aimed at forming parish BIA teams/accompaniers.*

Start-point 3 (SP3): IRS plan for the session with parent/parents

This start-point gives you a process to follow when an immediate response is needed and will help you plan your time with parents. It will give you a structure for your accompaniment. The SP3 MEET process will help you plan what to do. Each meeting with parents will need to be planned carefully but you will also need to be completely flexible in your framework of support. If the pastoral need arises and you have little time for planning, you can begin this start-point immediately. However, developing a team at the same time will be important. While accompanying parents, you should also invite some people from your team to focus on some of the leads from SP1 (raising the awareness of your parish community/ service) and SP2 (forming a team). *This stage is aimed at supporting and accompanying parents in times of immediate need.*

The MEET process SP1

Parish/chaplaincy development: fostering a *BIA* approach in your service or parish community

M: **Meet** the pastoral need: accompanying parents who receive the diagnosis of a pre-birth medical condition and possible experience of disability.

E: **Explain** the pastoral situation to your parish team and raise awareness of the *BIA* approach to accompaniment.

E: **Explore** the pastoral need; read through and become familiar with the *BIA* content and explore how you can raise the awareness of your parish.

T: **Transcend** by gathering all of the information you have explored and create a plan of action. Make plans for your *BIA* journey. Recruit volunteers who will be accompaniers.

Meet:

- Meet the pastoral need of parents and become familiar with Christian teaching surrounding the life of the child; engage with the *BIA* resources.

- Using chapters 1 and 2, meet your own approach to the life and faith story of a person who is disabled. Undertake a review of attitudes towards disability in your parish/chaplaincy. Notice the way in which you think about disability and the language you use.

- Review how welcoming and accessible the parish/chaplaincy is and whether it is underpinned by a positive or negative attitude towards the life and story of people who are disabled.

- Meet with the pastoral team/parish council and reflect upon the witness your service gives to the gift of life and promise of belonging. What promise do you offer? This should allow you to undergo a survey of your present services, practices and culture.

Explain:

Having undertaken the first stage:

- Explain the *BIA* approach to the parish community. You can do this by placing posters in your church, sermons, prayer groups, publications, coffee mornings. Using the *BIA* approach, you could plan activities that will raise awareness of disability and reflect hope and belonging.

- Also use creative methods to explain *BIA*: parish council agenda items, sections in your newsletters, inclusion in your programmes of lay formation, focused talks and additions to homilies.

- Explain how people with disabilities belong to the parish community and that their lives are important. Disability should be a necessary and ordinary engagement in all that a parish/chaplaincy does and provides. The *BIA* approach should be embedded into your programmes of marriage preparation. In this way potential parents will have a positive approach to the wonder of all life; they will be informed by Christian teaching. Such an approach will help all parents reflect upon the roads that they, or others, may travel in their lives. It becomes an ordinary way of life, a usual way of thinking and rippling *scintilli* of grace into the parish community.

Explore:

In the light of the *BIA* approach:

- Explore the physical, spiritual, formational and liturgical services of your church and how they would disable or enable a person or the family. Based on what you have learnt from the overview of services, make a plan of action.

- Recruit two or more volunteers who are willing to accompany parents who have received a pre-birth diagnosis. Where possible, this should include parents who have travelled a similar journey and who can empathise and accompany from within a lived experience. It is very important that the people recruited are able to act in a way that does not judge but holds a person's story with love and empathy. You are not looking for experts but for people who can befriend in a way that is non-judgemental and not overzealous.

- Try to recruit men who can empathise with the experience of a husband/father. This is very important.

Transcend:

Collate and move forward:

- Gather the names and details of people who may join as a group of accompaniers.

- Based on the *BIA* approach, the theological underpinning and what you have learned from the *BIA* parents' and parish resource, share information with your team.

- You should use the directives for being active listeners, found in chapter 3.

- Decide upon the location in which you will hold the BIA training session.

- Advertise that you will be starting the group and ask the parish to pray for the journey. No one involved should feel alone and all should feel supported.

- Plan to run a *BIA* programme of formation, ensuring that time for prayer is part of all you do together.

Insights from *BIA* parents concerning the importance of parish accompaniment

While still pregnant, "my faith community went above and beyond, visited me and helped us to plan a beautiful funeral for our daughter".

"I felt unable to make any decisions, I wanted someone with the knowledge of God to help me… thanks to the spiritual and practical support we received in the hard times we are still together and trying to find God's love in all of this… trying to see there is a space in the Church for us!"

"It helped me to understand some of the positions of the Church I am not familiar with, as well as challenge some of my deep-set preconceptions, but mostly it was reassuring to know that they [the parish team] were always there to support us and that they cared deeply for us."

It is the responsibility and the joy of the parish community to make an ordinary space in their services for God's accompaniment to be expressed in the delicate journey that parents must take.

The MEET process SP2

BIA programme of formation

M: **Meet** the people who have agreed to be accompaniers.

E: **Explain** the *BIA* approach and pathways and invite them to join the programme of preparation.

E: **Explore** the *BIA* approach and the accompaniers' thoughts regarding how to support parents. Explore the pathways and personal reactions of the team.

T: **Transcend** by agreeing on how you will run your parish programme, what IRS you will use and what support mechanisms you will develop. Set up a prayer rota and activities.

As workers in the vineyard we are all called to support one another. It is vital that from the very onset of this journey everyone involved agrees that they will work from the premise of accompaniment and support. Ministry is sustained by experiences of God's touch in times that are joyous and those that are sad. The *BIA* model of formation is one that holds Christ as our guide, leading you to sustain each other with love. Commitment to the journey, its content and process is vital if parents are to be accompanied in a way that will make a difference to their experiences. Accompaniers will also "have a personal and spiritual life which needs to be nourished, supported and encouraged";[30] it is therefore important that prayerful reflection is part of your journey together.

Before you begin the MEET of SP2:

- You should identify one person who will agree to be the *BIA* lead mediator; this could be a priest/minister or chaplain and can be adapted if the situation does not arise in the context of a parish community.

- The *BIA* lead mediator should become familiar with the *BIA* approach, resources and also the parents' book. The lead mediator will be responsible for setting up the programme of formation.

- The lead mediator should identify the sections of the *BIA* resources that will form a training session, following directives in the *BIA* parish resource.

- Special attention should be given to chapter 6 of the *BIA* parents' resource.

Each parish or setting will have their own creative ways of organising the programme of *BIA* formation. The team will choose the content for the course, according to the knowledge, understanding and experience of the people who have been recruited. The *BIA* resources will provide you with the rich content that you will need for your conversations. The MEET structure will give the framework for making the decisions. *BIA* invites you to be creative and motivated in developing resources and activities that you feel will enable you to accompany in pastoral situations.

SP2 MEET process in your setting with a particular attention to the Explore and Transcend sections

The lead mediator should:

Meet:

- Meet with the parish minister and the people who have agreed to join the team.

- Get to know each other's story and experience they have to share.

- Invite people to offer some of the skills that they have. You can be creative in gathering this information. Invite accompaniers to list the skills they feel are needed and then match skills to needs.

- Meet the *BIA* programme, the purpose of the journey, its content and develop desired outcomes of such a project.

- Meet with team and make plans for prayer times and for your formation programme.

Explain:

- Explain the *BIA* approach. This should be done by the lead mediator or pastor. You can just read it out from the *BIA* resource if needs be.

- Explain the four roads that parents might travel (using chapter 4 of the *BIA* parish resource or chapter 6 of the *BIA* parents' resource) and invite accompaniers to offer some immediate reactions or similar experiences.

- Explain the guidelines for active listening and the need for absolute confidentiality (information found in chapter 3).

- Explain what you feel the parish offers and ask the accompaniers to explain what more they feel might be needed for the project and what they are able to offer.

- Explain the importance of listening and creating space for parents to express themselves and have their story held and nurtured in confidentiality and love.

- Explain the prayer plan you will have developed at the Meet stage.

Explore:

This section will involve you making plans and be the most time-intensive.

- Explore the *BIA* approach in more depth. Spend time with your team deciding how you will run *BIA* in your parish.

- Explore the reactions and emotions of the accompaniers to the content shared.

- Explore what creative activities you can plan for; these could include family meals, visits to a park or another social activity, or something that will allow parents to shift from negative emotions or information they may have received through diagnosis.

- Explore how the new family might gain a deep sense of belonging in the parish and how you can place belonging at the centre of your accompaniment. Explore how you can affirm the child's value and assure the parish will welcome the family, wherever their pathway may lead.

- Consider the timetable you will need for meetings and team development.

- Discuss how you will support one another and what prayer activities you will develop for the parents and for you as a team.

- Consider where you will meet and what that would look like.

- Explore how you will provide an IRS.

- Discuss how you will accompany after hospital meetings and who would be available in times when immediate pastoral support is needed.

- Explore how you can be supportive in the *BIA* birth plan.

- Discuss how the parents can access parish services once the baby is born.

- Explore how you will support bereavement.

- Explore what your format/language/rubrics will be for a: baptism in state of emergency; memorial liturgy; funeral.

Transcend:

At this stage your plans should be in place and you should be ready to accompany parents.

- Put the information you have been exploring into a plan of action.

- Write up your plan of action (you can use the SP3 MEET planner).

- Decide where you will meet.

- Advise accompaniers of meetings, activities and timetable of events, including shared prayer times.

- With the parents' consent, invite the parish to accompany their journey with prayer and welcome.

- Do not offer judgement or advice, just be ready to listen, hold stories and accompany. Giving your time is the most precious gift that you can give for this precious gift of life in your parish.

- Meet with parents, accompany according to the *BIA* approach and share with them when and how they need you to.

- Help parents with research, resources and information for the future.

- Ensure continuation of accompaniment beyond the term of pregnancy which should help in issues of loss and memorials.

The MEET process SP3: accompanying parents and child on their journey (following SP1, SP2 or as an IRS)

M: **Meet** the parents and their unborn child.

E: **Explain** the *BIA* approach, the commitment of accompaniers and ask them to explain the pathways that they are on.

E: **Explore** the family's story, their needs, how the *BIA* approach can accompany their story. Work as a team and explore thoughts regarding how to support parents. Explore the pathways and personal reactions of the team.

T: **Transcend** by agreeing with parents how you will support their immediate needs. Accompany family.

Immediate Response Strategy (IRS)

As we have identified above, SP3 would ideally follow *BIA* SP1 and SP2. However, if there is an urgent need for support you should immediately initiate SP3.

The MEET process will give you all of the leads that you need to make plans and it will help you set up an initial encounter with parents and their unborn child.

Once the first meeting has taken place, you should follow the MEET process and become familiar with the parents' pathway, the *BIA* approach and how to apply it within the MEET framework. You should agree a pastoral plan for the parents' journey.

The *BIA* lead mediator should:

Meet:

- Meet parents who have been given the news of pre-birth diagnosis and possible disability. They may have only just received the news and you may meet them after they have visited the parish/service. This may require IRS. Without judgement and with love, listen and attend to their story.

- Meet the needs they have and discern the support you will begin to prepare for.

- Meet the *BIA* pathway that you feel the parents are travelling.

- Meet with volunteers whom you have been able recruit. Plan to meet with them separately so that they can follow a session of *BIA* preparation. If they have not been formed (SP2), invite them to read through the *BIA* parents' book.

- Meet the extended family who may also need to be part of the support network you develop. The extended family should meet the *BIA* approach so that you all accompany from the same start-point.

Explain:

- Explain and affirm the parents' important place of belonging and that you wish to accompany them with love.

- Ask them to share their story with you and receive it with gentleness. It will be very important to listen and not to offer advice (please see active listening guidelines in chapter 3).

- Gently explain the *BIA* approach and how this underpins the way in which they will be accompanied.

- Invite parents to talk about how they feel, to share the real concerns and issues they feel they are facing.

- Give the parents the *BIA* parents' book and prayer diary. Explain how the book might help them on their journey.

- Explain Christian teaching on the dignity of life and affirm your belief that their child is created in the image of God (found in chapter 4 of the *BIA* parents' resource). Remove disabling language such as "something being wrong with the child". No gift of life can ever be wrong because all life is good. We receive all life with love, for that is how it has been given.

- Explain the *BIA* approach to grandparents and support them as they travel with their children and unborn grandchild.

- Explain all of the services that the parish makes available for disabled people so as to enable their faith. This will give parents hope for the future and a sense of belonging to the "ordinary" activities of the parish.

- Encourage parents to use their prayer diaries and to explore their journey with grace.

- Be sure to help parents mark the child's existence and you could accompany them with prayer as they possibly give their child a name.

- Give parents images of children/adults with disabilities who have received the sacraments or who are active in the parish. Please try to show the parents that yours is a "parish of always" and that welcome and a space to grow are not just welcomed but belong to who you are (you will need to use elements of SP1 and 2 here).

Explore:

- Explore ever further all that the parish offers and all that could be available for the life of the child who is growing in the womb.

- Explore the equality policies of the medical service in which the parents are receiving care. Become familiar with their directives on meeting spiritual needs. Help the family to be confident when talking about their issues of belief and the unborn life of their child.

- Explore the hopes and expectations of the parents and family.

- With gentle enthusiasm, support the family in exploring moments of grace along their pathway; if their child is in danger of death, accompany gently. Please refer to the information on dealing with grief in chapter 3.

- With support and love, with empathy and a gentle compassion, explore the palliative/ bereavement care that can be made available to the family. You can use activities and prayers that we have suggested in this resource. You could create your own as a team.

- Explore how the family wish to pray with you; you could use their *BIA* prayer diary together if they wish.

- Explore the counselling services that are available to the parents.

- Assist the parents in exploring various support groups that they might benefit from, information on websites that might help.

- Explore the needs of the extended family and explore how you might support them further. Explore how parents could have some time off together; this is especially important if the parents have other children.

Transcend:

- Contact parents and give them the timetable of meetings according to what you have decided together.

- Continue to spend time listening and attending to their story.

- Continue to listen to their hopes and their fears and support them as they travel.

- Ensure that parish services are accessible and that your words and accompaniment are authentic.

- Accompany parents along their pathway; do not judge; and help parents to feel that they are valued and accompanied

- When accompanying parents along Pathway 3, please be sure that you read through the Christian teaching surrounding termination. Remember that parents do everything for love for their child and will need gentle accompaniment as they journey.

- Implement your session plan (see p. 84) and build the awareness of the parish community.

- Work with the hospital chaplain and the family regarding birth plans and programmes for palliative care.

- Accompany parents according to your plan and gently encourage them to notice *"scintilli* of grace", moments where God reaches into their life.

- Develop a prayer plan to follow with the parents and unborn child.

The **MEET** process above gives you the leads that you will need as you accompany; however, each situation will be individual and will need a flexible approach. The **MEET** process allows you to remove and replace some of our leads so that it can meet your particular pastoral context. On p. 84 is a **MEET** template to help you plan your sessions with parents.

BIA accompaniment session plan

Meet Where will you meet? Who will meet parents? Gather parents and meet their story; begin your session with prayer.	
Explain What information will you need to have ready so as to explain the *BIA* approach? Spend some time gently explaining the *BIA* approach.	
Explore Give parents time to explore the approach with you. Make sure parents have time and space to explore their feelings, Christian teachings, beliefs and life with their unborn child. What "accompanying" activities will you engage in? How will they help you explore the *BIA* pathway that parents are travelling?	
Transcend Pray with parents and their unborn child. Help parents to feel accompanied and that they are not alone. How will you do this? How will you pray?	

In this chapter we have explored how to set up a *BIA* journey in your faith community, noting the leads that you will need to follow so as to undertake journeys of accompaniment. This provides you with a framework but cannot cover all pastoral situations that may arise. The most important feature of the *BIA* journey is that you allow grace to enter into the relationship that you develop with the parents. Your approach must always affirm the gift of existence found in the presence of the unborn child. In moments that are challenging, it may feel that God is not present; however, these are moments when we are called to watch for God's presence and be with Christ. Recognising and feeling the presence of Jesus, in our human stories, helps us to realise that in all things we are never alone; through uniting our lives with Christ's we are always held in God's love.[31] This is the essence of the Christian story and must be one of the most active features of your journeys of Christian accompaniment.

In our next chapter we will bring all of the features of the *BIA* journey into a conversation with the life and human experience of Christ. We will introduce the "Living Fully" charter (Appendix) and invite you to place its principles at the heart of your mission as a Christian in the world.

CHAPTER FIVE

LIVING FULLY WITH GOD

BIA is a journey of Christian accompaniment for children and parents who receive a pre-birth diagnosis of a medical condition or possible experience of disability. During our time together, we have faithfully explored how we can share the promise of God with others. In the covenant God assures us that "I will adopt you as my own people, and I will be your God" (Exodus 6:7). This covenant proclaims that we belong to God and God belongs to us; we are made for each other. Our conversations, as we have introduced the *BIA* journey, have looked honestly at some of the issues that face babies with a pre-birth diagnosis, alongside the heart-rending and painful journeys of their parents. We have sought to bring their story and your own story into a reflective dialogue with the life of Christ, as shared through the Christian tradition. It has been a journey with God, a journey that we now hope you will repeat in your own parish setting. Through the testimony of the *BIA* parents and experience of the author we have met, explained and explored some of the cultural and religious dilemmas that parents may face as they live though their very human story. As we have accompanied each other, prayerful exchanges between "culture, tradition and experience"[32] have occurred. We have become attentive to God's gaze and the way in which God touches our lives and redeems them with love.

Remembering our story: a place to belong

Within the Christian tradition the Bible forms a book of witness which, page after page, retells the stories of lived experiences. It shares the stories of ordinary people who live out their lives faithfully, constantly seeking to encounter God. You could say that, as we engage in reading scripture and reflecting upon God's story, we are engaging in "faith seeking understanding";[33] we live so that we may discover our purpose, our vocation. God's promise of belonging draws every person into God's desire to touch our life, to be with us. Our God knows each of us, just as we are: "You know me through and through, from having watched my bones take shape when I was being formed in secret, knitted together in the limbo of the womb" (Psalm 139:15). As we scroll through the book of Genesis we are witness to a God who recognises the potential of all that God has created, including the diversity of the human person. "Here is the sign of the Covenant I make between myself and you and every living creature with you for all generations" (Genesis 9:12). The relationship God sought to establish with all God's people was not momentary; it was an everlasting promise of love and nobody is excluded from that. As you initiate a programme of Christian accompaniment you enable this promise to ripple into the lives of the people who need to know God's company and love. You become Christ's heartbeat.

Retelling our story: the human person in the image of God

Stories hold the potential of drawing us into "the reality and colours of each other's lives, through… shared joys and challenges", they "become a way to care".[34] In our time together, we have cared about the story of disabled people who often feel that they are a disappointment to the world and life of their families. This, however, is contested by a Christian vision of the human person as a wonderful sign and image of God (Psalm 139:14), who touches our life and the world through the body of each person. God gazes upon each human person with love and is amazed by creation (Genesis 1:26-28). God invites each person to return God's gaze, to be constantly drawn into God's company so as to participate fully in God's love and care for our life. To do this we need to learn how we might turn towards God as we encounter some of the sadness and joys that are, naturally, part of our human existence. We learn how to do this through God's ultimate gift of himself, in the person of Jesus, through whom God empathises and shares in our stories; through Christ, God accompanies our lives and offers salvation. God knows what it is like to suffer.

"Yes, God loved the world so much that he gave us his only Son, so that everyone who believes in him may not be lost but may have eternal life. For God sent his Son into the world not to condemn the world, but so that through him the world might be saved" (John 3:16-17).

Recalling our story: a very human life

"Jesus of Nazareth lived an ordinary human life":[35] he was conceived, he lived as a child, he experienced being part of a family, he ate, he slept, he shared in people's stories and accompanied many people as they travelled through their life. However, "his human life had a divine significance… what God spoke, Jesus lived",[36] and we have shared in God's Word as he "was made flesh, he lived among us" (John 1:14). In our *BIA* journey with parents, we invested time to learn from the human story of Jesus, by entering imaginatively into the story of the parents, Joseph and Mary, who were chosen to accompany his life. As we travelled with them on their unexpected pathway, we noticed how God the Father both calls and transforms their lives through the life of his unborn child. As we travel within the experience and traditions of these three faith-filled people, entwined with the lived experiences and insights of our *BIA* parents, we explore how biblical images can quite "mysteriously evoke the depths of our inner story".[37] Through "entering a scene from Jesus' life"[38] we are invited to reflect upon our own life with God. As you plan to run a *BIA* journey in your parish, or as you accompany parents, rely upon the words of God by sharing times of prayer. Help parents and their unborn child to be with God in prayer.

Reviving our story: a journey with love

We have noted, as we have travelled though the *BIA* resources, how unexpected roads can be painful. The unplanned pathway, which Mary and Joseph agreed to follow, threw them into confusion. It took them on a journey that was totally human yet totally divine. God enters into their story and in response to God's grace they agreed to allow their human hearts to beat with Christ's. They accepted all of the differences that came with the conception, life and death of the Christ child. Through Mary and Joseph's acceptance of God's call we are given Christ; they became a witness to all that is made possible when travelling with God. Mary and Joseph's very human story assures us of God's company, of God's gaze upon us and that God's heart beats with ours.

Jesus is the heartbeat of God; he was conceived, grew in the womb and was born with a mission to reveal God to us. This is what we believe to be a Christian truth, that through Christ we can encounter God. Jesus' ability to do God's work and live as God's gift relied upon Mary and Joseph's willingness to travel through the sufferings and joys of human existence. They were asked to accompany Christ through birth, life, death and finally to his resurrection and the redemption of life itself. As Christians this is a call to all of us and one that the parents you accompany are truly living. They are witnesses in time, accompanying their child's life with love and relying upon God. As they struggle with the emotions and realities of their unexpected pathway, they grapple with God; they are truly living their faith and our joy is to acknowledge and thank them for the witness they give.

Living fully with Christ: a Christian witness

"Faith is not merely something that human beings achieve; it is what configures our humanity."[39] It shapes who we are and how we live. As Christians we are asked to live in a certain way. Our faith does not only shape each individual person, it forms who we are as a people of God and asks us to witness to a radical story of love. We are called to evidence the teachings of Christ, who, throughout his human story, showed us how to lovingly approach each and every person. Jesus developed a "culture of encounter"[40] rather than one of exclusion, revealing to us that the promise of God was real. Jesus met with people of all abilities, indeed he made an even greater effort to meet people whom society rejected.

He brought their story into the very centre of his own. The words and actions of Jesus and his call to friendship become a lens into the very mystery of God, into the story of humans, and as such we receive instructions for how we should love and value each other as equals. Persons who are disabled are much like any other person. They have stories, experiences, ideas, knowledge and emotions to share. They work, they laugh, they suffer, they marry, they have children, they live and participate fully in God's promise of belonging, just because they are and as they are. Christ includes the whole of humanity when he tells us, "I have come so that they may have life and have it to the full" (John 10:10).

"The person with disabilities is, with all the very many people, entrusted to the Church's care. Just like all God's children, the person with disabilities comes into this world to know Him, to love Him and to serve Him and so to come to Paradise."[41]

Conclusion: because I am

It is this entrusting of each life that underpins the Christian Church's constant defence of the dignity of every human life. This is sometimes in stark contrast to a medical and mechanical way of approaching the body. The pre-birth diagnosis of a disability presents the life of a person, not a stereotype that society has developed. Negative response to such people's presence can be the immediate offer of termination. This seems to suggest that their lives would be of less value, and as such they really should not be around, and lays bare the "secret [and somewhat eugenic] thoughts of many" (Luke 2:35). Disabled people's lives can be enshrined in negative language and they can often be in danger of being "objects of pity and opportunities to grow in sanctification".[42] As Christians, however, we are called to reject these negative images set up by cultures and to learn from Christ's example of encounter; we are asked to witness to the mystery of life, of living fully just as we are. As we enter into the story of Christ, we mirror what he said, how he lived; we witness to and celebrate the dignity of human life, as together we make up the body of Christ. What God spoke Jesus lived, what Jesus showed we are called to do; we have learnt how to live our lives. Jesus helps us to know how to keep our gaze securely on God, how to be accompanied in the rises and the falls of life. We are supported as we weather the experiences of rejection that Simeon so powerfully suggested would be part of Jesus' vocation: "You see this child: he is destined for the fall and for the rising of many… destined to be a sign that is rejected" (Luke 2:34).

In the story of the presentation of Christ, Mary encounters Simeon at the entrance of the Temple, at the door of a faith community. His words come as a shock to both parents, as he tells Mary that "a sword will pierce your own soul" (Luke 2:35). Following this encounter, with such a painful piece of information, Mary must have felt very anxious about the life of her newborn child. I wonder if she will have spent the rest of her son's life waiting: waiting for suffering to come, waiting for him to be rejected. Jesus, we can see from this, knows what it is like to be different. His companions in life, Mary and Joseph, know what it is like to live with difference and as such they share in the story of the many thousands of parents who, throughout time, have given life to people who are then disabled. However, Mary and Joseph were never left alone in their deeply human journey. Along their pathway, there were always moments where other people made a difference to their life with Christ. As Jesus grew, in the safety of the womb, Mary and Joseph's journey was enriched by people who accompanied and loved them, who accepted and rejoiced in the presence of their son. These occasions of graceful accompaniment happened again and again, both before and after Jesus' birth, into his life, just before his death and flowing into his resurrection. As Jesus' life came to an end, we find him on the cross, steeped in pain as he recognises the need for accompaniment in suffering. Keeping his gaze upon the people who had faithfully accompanied his life, he looked at his mother and the disciple he loved, ensuring that they would not be left alone: "'Woman, this is your son'. Then to the disciple he said, 'This is your mother'" (John 19:26-27). Jesus felt the reality of suffering death. In all our anxieties and fears, we are never alone. Through Christ, we encounter a God who knows what it means to be separated from a child, and to have that child rejected. Our suffering matters to God, and this is why the resurrection of Christ moves us all from suffering to life, for, as Jesus lived, God redeemed. This is the story of our salvation; it is our salvation history.

"As Christians we are called to be witnesses of the resurrection,"[43] we are called to witness to the fact that beyond all our unexpected experiences of anxiety, of death, of change, there is life. This is the promise of Christ. Following his resurrection, we continue to witness God's care for God's people. God's promise of never leaving us alone continues to build the culture of encounter that I have suggested is so important in the mission of Christ, and, I would add, in your *BIA* journey. Knowing the fear and sense of loss that his disciples would feel, Jesus continues to be present in their lives, re-entering their lives so that they may move forward, no matter what happens. "After the resurrection Jesus appeared to his disciples to confirm that he had risen,"[44] so that all the sadness and fear that they had experienced throughout his crucifixion could be redeemed by love. Once again Jesus teaches us to live faithfully through the witness and stories of these men and women of faith. In the same way he re-enters our own story, time and time again, after each rise and each fall. Jesus wishes to offer everybody an "experience of his resurrection",[45] reassuring us, as he did his disciples, that we will never be alone: "I shall ask the Father, and he will give you another Advocate to be with you for ever" (John 14:16). As you now move on to run *BIA* journeys of Christian accompaniment, you are promised the Spirit of God; this Spirit will show you how to move forward when life has proved hard. "A Christian life is where grace becomes real and actual,"[46] it is where God gracefully touches our life and redeems it. It is where we can find peace. As you travel through your truly human and Christian story with parents you are asked to help them to rest in God's peace, trust in our God and allow God's teaching and promise to guide you all.

Your accompaniment: a truly Christian story

In the story of Jesus, we find that "diversity has become a new norm and living faithfully in the world is the expected way of being in the world".[47] The world of today is truly changing and disabled people, who enjoy diversity in their body and creative ways of learning, have begun to live as God designed. Their witness "challenges those who think that a disabled life is not worth living by the way in which they can live fully, in celebration of hope".[48] Professor Reinders reminds us that "The way in which we experience illness and disability is an index of the love we are ready to offer."[49] Each gift of life, therefore, is a sign of God's life. It is an invitation to love as Christians, to abandon measurements of the body and to create an index of love that "the world cannot give" (John 14:27). We are asked to love as God loves, to do as Christ did and to "respond to this gift in a life of faithful stewardship [and] care"[50] of one another. We are called to welcome and love because we have first been welcomed and loved by God, from the moment of our own conception and for the whole of our life. It is with this love that the *BIA* parents and programme seek to accompany parents on their journeys with their child from our first moment of encounter and for the whole of their life. Their child, present in the womb, lost to us in death, or given to us in the richness of his or her diversity, brings new energy and witness to the Christian story. The child brings an unrepeatable dignity that colours and enriches the body of Christ, to which we all belong and from which nobody can be excluded. This is the promise of God, it is offered freely to all people, it is offered to you and to all the children of God. The unborn child is a valued member of the body of Christ just because he or she is. Along with John Oliver, whose story we heard at the start of our journey, the child can claim from within his or her own being that he or she belongs to God and the world "just because I *am*".

As we draw to the end of our time together may we invite you to put all that we have shared into practice, living fully with God. In the Appendix to this resource, you will find the "Living Fully" charter, which we have referred to throughout our journey. Please read through it and use it to guide your practice and parish commitment to Christian love and the building of wonderful communities. Invite as many people as you can to sign up to its vision and practise its message. May we close by offering you our promise of accompaniment, "of our unity and solidarity through love".[51] Thank you for your witness as Christian accompaniers, for the commitment you give to unborn children and their parents, helping them teach the world and the Church to love.

"Trust in Christ, listen to him, follow his ways. He never abandons us, not even in the darkest moments of our lives. He is our hope, the Church is not distant from your trials, but it accompanies you with love. God is close to you and accompanies you by the hand. Look towards him in the most difficult moments and he will give you consolation and hope. Trust yourselves to his love"[52] (Pope Francis).

We would like to give the last word of our *BIA* journey to the voice of the child in the womb. This is a reflective message that was revealed through prayer, the author's reflection on her own story, that of the *BIA* parents and the story of the unborn Christ.

This prayer acknowledges and celebrates the gift of life.
It reflects the _BIA_ approach.[53]

With God I was breathed into being.

I am enfolded in God's presence and I am here,

I have been here, Because I am and will always be a gift.

I have heard the voices and the tears, I have felt the hope and the

despair... for I am here... because I am God's loving creation

I ask only that I am accompanied and loved, that I make you feel proud.

It is good to cry for it shows the depth of your love but never regret my
being here.

Never feel cheated by my presence and I pray that "because I am",
I bless you as I respond to God's call with my life .

My life may be short or long but I know you

have loved me for the whole of my life

this is my call... the vocation my life calls you to...

to love... never anger...

let my life not bring regret...

love must be loved.

Because I am

pure gift.[54]

96

ACKNOWLEDGEMENTS

"No pastoral visit brings wholeness. No programme accomplishes the Church's mission. No set of goals and objectives includes everything. This is what we are about. We plant the seeds that one day will grow. We water seeds already planted, knowing that they hold future promise. We lay foundations that will need further development. We cannot do everything, and there is a sense of liberation in realising that. It may be incomplete, but it is a beginning, a step along the way, an opportunity for the Lord's grace to enter and do the rest." (Bishop Ken Untener, "In Memory of Oscar Romero", from a homily by Cardinal John Dearden, 1979)

This prayer accompanies me in my work as a practical theologian. It always reminds me that nothing is achieved in isolation; pastoral ministry is collaborative. The development of the *BIA* pastoral programme is indeed founded upon the collaboration of many people, whom I wish now to acknowledge and thank. *BIA* emerged from a conversation with Stefania Prandelli, the gifted artist whose beautiful illustrations have brought life to my words; I thank her in awe and wonder of her talents. I am eternally grateful to Gill Chaddock, her patience and diligence in helping me to write and proofread is the bedrock of all my work; thank you for being such a generous and important friend. The content of *BIA* is the fruit of many people's stories, of conversations with colleagues, of reflection with God and is built on the insights of others; this is especially true of Giada Vincenzi, who started me thinking about how to support the lives of unborn, disabled children and their family. *BIA* cannot do everything, but I would like to thank the people who have helped me to take a step along the way, making space for God's promise to be recognised in people's lives. I would like to thank Nicole Barber and Fr Denis McBride C.Ss.R.; as publishers your patience and pastoral support have been moments of grace. To the families who have shared their journeys with me, I am eternally grateful: Ewelina, Plamen and their son Karl; Becky, Gerard and their daughter Aurelia; my son Claudio, daughter-in-law Charlotte and my grandson Giorgio; Martin, Sergio, Adrian, June – thank you. I hope I have been faithful to your stories. For Monsignor Jim Curry, thanks to your pastoring, our conversations and shared journey have been touched by true grace and love.

My gratitude also goes to colleagues in the Pontifical Council for Culture, for believing in the lives and faith of disabled people and for leading us to "Live Fully". My sincere gratitude goes to his eminence Cardinal Gianfranco Ravasi, for your patronage of our work; to Monsignor Melchor Sanchez de Toca and Monsignor Gergely Kovacs for your prayers and friendship; they sustain our mission.

The writing and development of any resource needs the gift of time and space; these I have received from the hospitality of the Carmelite community in Rome. Fr Míceál O'Neill, and Fr Kevin Alban, you have not only given Kairos space to work, you are in every word I write, thank you. Fr Edmundo, your gift of Pope Francis' words pours courage and witness into the lives of the people who will travel with *BIA*. To all my brothers at CISA, thank you. Receiving the precious gift of time and conviction from colleagues is what I thank my friends at Livability for: Adam Bonner, Mat Ray and Janet Miles; it has all added up, thank you. I would also like to thank my colleagues from the field of disability theology whose work and wisdom feed me daily and which is found on every page of this resource. The foundations of my pastoral mission lay in the work of Pia Matthews, John Swinton and Hans Reinders, who have led a world of theologians and practitioners. Pia, thank you for being my mentor and guide, your work on the human person in the eyes of God feeds us all; your encouragement is the reason I write. John, thank you for your unmeasurable knowledge; your work is a gift to us all, thank you also for the laughter. Hans, thank you for the gift of friendship, it has "watered" my work and this pastoral resource. I also acknowledge with gratitude the pastoral, honest and thorough debates of John Wyatt. His guidance through issues of life and death in the Christian tradition and the personal support he gave us for a pastoral need has formed this resource.

The vineyard of disability theology is filled with passionate and diligent workers, all of whom reflect and pastor with great love. The conversations and academic studies of my fellow "workers" have underpinned the content and practices of *BIA*. I would therefore like to thank my conversation partners, community and friends who have provided a harvest from the field. To Liam Waldron; Liam, you inspire and teach me, thank you. Anne Masters, you help me to live fully and hopefully. Sister Veronica Donatello and Luca Badetti, *siete la mia anima e catechesi*, my catechists of the soul. Baroness Sheila Hollins, your generosity and scholarship goes beyond words. Zach Duke, your depth is the promise for our future. To Roy McCloughry, thank you for our "enabled" stories. To Talitha Cooreman, thank you for your knowledge so freely shared; and Medi Volpe, thank you for giving us the wisdom of your life with Anna and with God. There are always people whose belief in your work enables it to grow: John Coleby is one such person. John, thank you for belief in Kairos as it supports families who receive a challenging pre-birth diagnosis. I would also like to thank Bill Gaventa and Miguel Romero; you accompany me, always, in all ways.

BIA is a harvest of stories, thoughts, academic studies, pastoral visits and conversations, undertaken as I have travelled into the life and mission of the Church. My hope is to have faithfully gathered the harvest so that it may become food for our shared journeys. To thank everyone who has helped me develop this resource would fill several more pages. I would like, therefore, to thank all of the pilgrims that I have met along the way, but most especially I would like to end with acknowledging the people who continually sustain and inspire me, practically and personally, you make it all possible.

To my friends in the Kairos Team, to Gill, Antoinette, Mike, Kathleen, Sean and Fred, thank you for the gift of your time and skills; you are what makes Kairos real and what helps it minister. To all my friends, you know who you are, thank you for helping me to be.

My family is the reason I am. My mother Josie, brother Frank, his wife Anne Marie, my sister Geraldine and her family put up constantly with my "comings and goings", rambling and constant requests for help; to you all, thanks! I love you. I would especially like to thank my sons Massimo, Luca and Claudio, together with my daughter-in-law Charlotte and grandson Giorgio; you are the joy in my life, my blessing and my grace, thank you for your generosity in always sharing me with others. Finally, I would like to thank God for the witness of Celine and Sister Lucia who have helped me recognise the presence of the Eucharist in our family, found in the "Am-ness" of my nephew Sebastian and grandson Giorgio. My life has been enriched by the presence of you all; I thank God for the wonder of who you are.

APPENDIX

THE LIVING FULLY CHARTER 2016

Please read through and share with the parish community as part of your disability awareness and parish formation.

Celebrating life and living fully

Statement from "Living Fully 2016: Disability, Culture and Faith – A Celebration"

Introduction

On 23-26 June 2016, in Rome, the Living Fully Symposium and Conference, co-hosted by the Pontifical Council for Culture and the Kairos Forum, brought together persons with disabilities, theologians, clergy, religious, families and laity for a four-day conference. We shared our stories, prayed together and explored the personal, pastoral and theological dimensions and implications of disability for people to live fully in the life of their congregations and communities. Our events identified the unique role and powerful witness that the Church can give in making "Living Fully"[55] possible for everyone. The presenters and delegates of the conference have developed the following statement that honours the reflections, discussions and themes that arose in the course of the four days. We hope it captures the expressions and voice of the hundred and sixty-five people who travelled from thirteen countries across the world to participate.

We believe that the Church plays a profound role in the ways that disability impacts and is impacted by all of the cultures in which the Church lives and serves.

Language

We recognise that language holds an important place in how the lives and stories of people are shared and discussed.[56]

We will use the terms "disabled persons" and "persons with disabilities" throughout this document for specific meanings. We acknowledge that negative language and a lack of access "disables" people, setting up physical, cultural and attitudinal barriers, which prevent living fully. Within this document we will use the term "disabled persons" to reflect this reality. However, people are first of all unique persons, worthy of God-given dignity. Disabling factors (physical, intellectual and/or emotional) may be a part of their lives, but "they are persons first". Within this document we will also use the term "persons with disabilities"[57] to reflect this reality. Additionally, we wish to acknowledge that some persons with disabilities prefer the reference "disabled persons". Though their disability is not all of their identity, they feel it is a part of it, which is claimed with this reference.[58]

It is a constant challenge to reject limiting labels, stereotypes and assumptions. Therefore, we ask readers to examine their own opinions and language, which contribute to social isolation and diminished expectations, these can be more limiting than physical impairments and inaccessible environments. We call on everyone to build communities where all people are supported and valued.

Context

Recent changes in thought and legislation across the world have thrown up significant challenges to traditional understandings of what disability means to the human person. The key issues identified for and by persons with disabilities are ones of rights, inclusion and participation. The vision is one of full and active participation, by persons with disabilities and their families, in their communities and society. The key implication for the Church's culture and practice is that we could and should be the leader in that full and active participation, due to our understanding and promoting of the dignity of the human person. As the body of Christ, the Church is called to move beyond issues of physical access and supportive care to an embodiment of the possibilities of "living fully" within both the Church and the culture in which it witnesses, evangelises and serves.

The aims of the conference

Living Fully 2016 provided a creative space to reflect upon how the experience and expressions of people might provide "new fields for evangelisation".[59] The gathering enabled us to ponder both theologically and practically on "the mystery of the world and in particular of the human person", with a particular focus on how we might provide a way to give "expression to the transcendent dimensions of human life",[60] where disability is present. The ever-growing field of Disability Theology provides an opportunity for all to encounter and explore the Gospel through the life experiences of persons with a disability, their families and loved ones. Living Fully 2016 initiated critical and hospitable conversations around the theological, pastoral and practical issues that are raised by the varied experiences of disability across contexts, faiths and cultures. Together, people with and without disabilities exchanged good practices, engaged in theological conversation, prayed, networked and celebrated the lives and faith of the delegates in all their diversity and giftedness.

Living Fully 2016: Disability, Faith, Culture and Practice – A Celebration

All life is gift: the rich diversity of the human story

Every human being is "created in the image of God".[61] In Christianity this is the essence of the gift of human life. The image of God is not a quality we earn but reflects the loving relationship that our heavenly creator maintains with each of us. Therefore, all human beings stand equal in their relationship with their Creator.[62] In Genesis God called the creation of human beings "very good".[63] God rejoices in diversity. Pope Francis reminds us that diversity is not something to fear but that "differences are precisely our wealth".[64] After all, "a world where everyone is the same would be a boring world".[65] Celebrating diversity is indeed a "way to improve, to be more beautiful and richer".[66]

Within this diverse human family created by and for God, every human being is precious (Psalm 139) and unique. As Cardinal Ravasi shared in his opening statement of the Living Fully symposium, "Every human being has both a physical aspect (*bios*[67]) and spiritual aspect (*zoe*).[68] These aspects make up the person's 'complex wholeness'." In both of these different aspects "the human being belongs to God's good creation and is holy".[69] However, when persons with disabilities are met by others, they are often only recognised in their physical or intellectual aspect, thus missing the person in his or her wholeness, missing the "wonder that is that unique human being".[70] There are other times when persons with disabilities have been romanticised as "God's special angels" who provide opportunities for "us" to grow in grace through helping "them". This "contradicts our call to see Christ in all, and to be Christ to my neighbour".[71] Further, it denies their humanity, setting the disabled persons apart from non-disabled persons, enhancing isolation and loneliness that is part of being human.[72] All people are created in the image of God and as such, there is no "them and us but only us".[73]

As proclaimed by the psalmist in psalm 139, all the delegates at Living Fully called for people to see every person as being "wonderfully made".[74] Our lives are not valuable because of the state or condition of our bodies and minds. "All are equally loved by God, which means that there is no norm that renders the lives of some human beings more valuable than others."[75]

As Pope Francis reminds us, "we must remove our sandals when we are on the holy ground"[76] of our "encounter with another person".[77]

Persons living with disability within the life, mission and culture of the Church

Christians are called to celebrate the gift of life in the Church and are, together, the body of Christ. As Christ's body, we must therefore mirror the way in which he met people and offered belonging within the kingdom of God. This sense of belonging was mirrored in the activities and vision of the Living Fully events, which included each and every person, no matter their presumed ability. When the Church forgets this and creates barriers for some to belong, "the Body of Christ is incomplete and does not reflect the whole image of God, it risks no longer being the Body of Christ".[78] Persons with disabilities are among those who experience multiple kinds of barriers that exclude, both attitudinal and architectural. Disability is also often correlated with lack of opportunity to contribute to society, poverty, hunger and adequate housing. A common experience of the delegates suggested that their personal "call to apostolic and missionary capacity" is often not recognised or facilitated. This can be due to a lack of knowing how to provide creative and "appropriate access"[79] for persons with disabilities in the life and mission of the Church. Pope Francis tells us, "There is widespread attention to disability in its physical, mental and sensory form." He also notes that whilst there is an ever increasing welcoming attitude, "our communities are still struggling to practise true inclusion and full participation in a way that is ordinary".[80] Living Fully 2016 recognised that when persons with disabilities and their families participate in the Church, they are not usually present or welcomed from a culture of belonging and active participation for all, that is, being part of the ordinary. Too often their participation is defined as something "special", and thus by definition still different.

At Living Fully 2016 the delegates felt that they were part of something where "EveryBody"[81] was together, where each person felt that they were expressing, themselves and their faith, within a culture of equality and belonging.[82] The common experience that emerged from the conference was that the presence of each person and their unique contribution was valued as an ordinary way of being Church together, and the expectation was "that everybody had something to bring".[83] Being part of a community that attends to the gifts of all, that listens, accepts and learns from each other was the common experience[84] of delegates. A Church where all people know their rightful place of belonging mirrors a culture of love and serves to "evangelise culture" by loving and valuing God and every single person from within whom they are born to be (Mark 12:30-31).[85] "Our sacred spaces can and must become our safe places."[86]

There are places where the Church lives out this call and vision in ways that profoundly impact its own congregations and the communities and culture in which they live. However, that is the exception, rather than the rule. Thus, the delegates of Living Fully 2016 have asked that we create a charter for the Church that all individuals, clergy and parishes can sign up to and use within their community, life and mission. We have created two: one that speaks more directly to the issues of theology and ecclesiology raised by the experience of disability, and a second that is in more inclusive language, reflecting the variety of voices and abilities present at this unique conference.

The Living Fully 2016 statement

The way forward – living an ordinary culture of belonging for all

This statement has emerged directly from the delegates of the Living Fully 2016 events and is directed to all of the world. The key recommendations highlighted in this statement are that:

We, the Church, affirm the uniqueness, dignity and value of each person as created in the image of God. We recognise that disabled people have an important role to play within the people of God, but do not always feel their importance to God because of hard hearts, lack of imagination and misdirected pity towards them. They must, therefore, be welcomed and enabled to enjoy a place of belonging where their lives and gifts are recognised, valued, facilitated and celebrated. In so doing, we, the Church, provide a profound contrast to cultures in which persons with disabilities and their families are too often neglected, isolated, excluded, and/or relegated to the margins of social and community life.[87]

We, the Church, recognise and honour the expressions, experiences, insights, wisdom and choices of persons with disabilities and their families, providing a model for culture, systems of care, social services and faith communities. The Church must learn from disabled people and their loved ones, and a space must be created to enable people to express their knowledge and faith in God. In so doing we all become evangelists to others and to culture.[88]

We, the Church, are willing to fully embrace the real experiences of persons with disabilities and their families, including the spiritual wounds that have been caused by neglect and/or exclusion from the Church itself. In so doing we will live out our collective call to "be the living Body of Christ",[89] reaching out to befriend, touch and welcome all in the Spirit of the living and risen Christ, learning the stories and needs of others.[90]

We, the Church, recognise the joys and graces that come from a culture of belonging, where diversity is celebrated within the communal and faith-filled life of the Church. In so doing, we, the Church, will facilitate a cultural shift and witness to the full body of Christ, which is enriched by all people who all, according to their way of being, enjoy access, belonging and contribution to the whole of that body (1 Corinthians 12). This will mirror the diversity of God's creation and the strengths inherent in the human spirit.

We, the Church, affirm the gifts of every person and desire that disabled persons enjoy their right and opportunity to use these gifts in praise and service to God. Delegates of Living Fully have asked that they are "treated the same as everyone else".[91] Living Fully repeats and agrees with the call of Pope Francis that our faith communities "welcome everyone or no one".[92] In so doing, the people of God offer a prophetic witness to the world, reaching out to all people and offering a place where human, spiritual and legal[93] rights can be lived to the full.[94]

We, the Church, honour the desire and capacity of persons with all forms of disability and their families to be in relationship with God, and to help lead others into prayer and worship. Disabled persons must be empowered to live out their personal call to discipleship and have important and valued roles within their faith communities. In so doing, the worship and witness of the Church serves to call every single person to respond to the gift and mystery of life at the heart of the Church's teachings and sacraments.[95]

We, the Church, recognise that attitudes, culture and practices in our faith communities and structures must change if we are to ensure a celebration of diversity.[96] Jesus himself spoke to this when he responded to the faith of friends who were willing to remove a roof for their friend to gain access to him (Mark 2:1-12).[97] As in Pentecost, we remain open to all forms of communication and we are open to be evangelised through it, amazed and surprised by one another, our stories and common journey of faith. In so doing differentiated communication and symbolic language will be creative and ordinary ways to communicate and will contribute to the formation of culture, faith and liturgy.[98]

We, the Church, ask that a culture of formation for clergy, religious and lay leaders and practitioners be developed and fostered that engages with prophetic insights[99] from the disciplines of disability and theology. In so doing, a culture will be established in which welcoming the lives and faith of persons with disabilities is an ordinary way of forming the practice and teachings of faith communities and traditions.[100]

Additional insights were expressed by delegates who are creative learners and who have personally dealt with the multiple dimensions of disability.

"I have so much to offer; receive it."

"Treat me like you do everyone else."

"Being together is good and inspires people to act."

"I am valuable: value me."

"Doing things together, with me not for me."

"Please be open to all forms of communication, be open to be evangelised through it, amazed and surprised by one another, our stories and common journey of faith."[101]

"It is a call to a culture of change, belonging and love."

"We can only live life to the full if we do it together, this is a model of community and mirrors what it means to be Church."[102]

Conclusion

The conference experienced what a "community of faith could look like", when persons with disabilities are valued and the community is confident that each person is "unique and unrepeatable, and any exclusion of any person would impoverish the community".[103]

Living Fully advocates that Christian communities should be "homes" where all who experience exclusion, isolation or disabilities, can feel understood, respected and valued.[104] As one delegate noted, the entranceway, the living room, and the dining space in a home, indicate growing degrees of welcome and hospitality. But at the heart of the home is the kitchen, where masks are lowered and love, presence and gifts are shared. We will make sure that all people are welcome within the "Kitchen of the Church"[105] where action and welcome is taking place, rather than being relegated to spaces in which the hospitality is less inclusive and real. This will happen when people are no longer disabled by lack of access and where together the wisdom, gifts and insights of all people, of all abilities, guide and enrich the body of Christ.

The delegates of Living Fully enjoyed a common experience where they were able to make friends[106] where they felt united within a culture of joy and celebration, yet also one that challenged each participant to recognise the ways that our own attitudes and practices need to change and grow. From within this experience, we have also developed a charter for the Church that is inclusive of the voices and expressions of everyone at the conference with varying levels of understanding and communication. We advocate that its vision becomes an ordinary way of fostering a culture of celebration and belonging, calling all to build the Church in faith, hope, and love.[107]

The charter

Living Fully within the Church

Because we are created in the image of God, we will:

- Show unconditional love; do as Jesus did, valuing all people of all abilities.

- Each be the glue that joins people together to celebrate themselves and their creation, no matter their body form and way of communicating.

- Show that each of us is loved by God, and that we are each and everywhere in the presence of God. We will be a witness for Christ and follow him.

- Celebrate being a Eucharistic people by enabling all to truly live out his/her vocation.

- Be creative artists in the work of God and in response to God's call, helping all to see and treat one another as unique individuals, each as God's work of art, rather than by labels that limit and exclude.

- Ensure that people of all abilities and disabilities feel invited, welcomed and received as full members of God's community.

- Commit to helping others find and experience their own innate sense of worth and belonging, because we bear the image of God, we are the body of Christ and we are inspired by holy scripture and the life of Jesus.

Because we are called to love all people, we will:

- Love God, love others, treat and serve everyone the same.

- Lead by example, seek positive change and foster a culture of justice and belonging.

- Help people to find peace and feel welcome in the Church.

- Reach out by invitation and welcome people from all over the world, especially people who have been disabled and excluded.

- Attend to, receive, listen and make time for persons with disabilities and their families to express their faith, needs, gifts and call to discipleship.

- Be evangelisers of all abilities: to EveryBody and with EveryBody.

- Together, develop creative skills in communication and access. Our faith communities will be accessible to all and a place of belonging for all.

We believe that the Church where persons with disabilities are present is:

- A place where creative ministry and friendship are an ordinary way of being together.

- A place where we "Live Fully" within a culture of belonging.

- A community of love, joy, welcome and an invitation to reflect the image of God in the world.

- A space to share in faith and grow in friendship.

- A community where all people can respond to their call to be a disciple of Christ and enjoy ministering and evangelising with others.

- A community where each person can live out their innate uniqueness and rightful place in the world and community of faith.

- A community that sees beyond the labels and sees the person, not the disability or impairment.

- A witness to love at the heart of the Church.

- A community "Living Fully" and giving witness to love in worship and service.

RESOURCES

CONTINUING ON YOUR JOURNEY

People with disabilities and their families are beginning to share their stories. This is providing us with a new approach to culture and encourages us to create new traditions for the future. All of the *BIA* parents mentioned how important it was for them to contact support groups and find information that could help the journey with their unborn child.

Below you will find some initial information that might help you. The Internet holds a sea of information so I have also put some key words in for you to use which might avoid you linking in to sites that are unsympathetic with the *BIA* approach. I have only one comment about most such sites and that is they often use deficit language, for example, "when we found out something was wrong". The *BIA* approach resists the use of such terminology for a person's life so we hope that by highlighting this for you it will help you notice and avoid any disabling cultures.

Some information you may find helpful

When looking for support networks you can use the following key words:

- Pre-birth support groups and disability

- Pre-birth diagnosis and pastoral care

- Positive access and disability

For an inspirational story for parents who have travelled the pathway *BIA* promotes, please research Chiara Corbella Petrillo.

Useful websites regarding support for pre-birth diagnosis and support

The Christian Medical Fellowship: www.cmf.org.uk

Petals: Counselling for pre-birth trauma in pregnancy: petalscharity.org

The story of being Noah's dad: noahsdad.com/story

Noah's Children (USA) hospice care: www.noahschildren.org

Best Beginnings: Parents' advocate and support: www.bestbeginnings.org.uk/parents-with-learning-disabilities

Lily's Gift (USA): a network of concerned parents and professionals who have experienced or worked closely with issues surrounding poor prenatal diagnosis: www.lilysgift.org

Embracing Grace: bioethics and support: www.cdrcmfl.org/respectlife/embracinggrace

Media links: sharing stories

Frank Stephens: "I Am a Man With Down Syndrome and My Life Is Worth Living": www.realclearpolitics.com/video/2017/10/31/frank_stephens_i_am_a_man_with_down_syndrome_and_my_life_is_worth_living.htm

People at Livability share about life and community: www.livability.org.uk/share-story-listening-service-users

Linda del Rio: Linda del Rio from the Jack del Rio foundation works tirelessly to share with people who experience disability. One of the projects she works with is called Mary's children. Their story is very inspiring and shows what can be achieved with a positive approach: maryschildrenfamilycenter.org

Useful Christian organisations regarding disability and faith community

The Kairos Forum: author's website, consultancy, disability, access and faith: www.thekairosforum.com

Christian disability groups: Churches for All is a network of Christian disability-focused organisations that works in partnership with Premier Life: churchesforall.org.uk

Looking to the future with hope: organisations that can help you now and in the future

Livability is the disability charity that connects people with their communities. The charity tackles social isolation and the barriers that can cause people to be disabled and vulnerable in their lives. Through a wide range of disability, education, training and community services, Livability promotes inclusion, belonging and wellbeing for all: "We put the elements in place that all add up to connected lives and communities": www.livability.org.uk

Books Beyond Words provides books and training to support people who find pictures easier to understand than words. Whether supporting somebody who has been intellectually disabled or who experiences communication difficulty, their products empower people through pictures: booksbeyondwords.co.uk

St Joseph's Pastoral Centre: A safe place for adults with intellectual disabilities to learn, recognising their gifts and talents and valuing their unique place in the world, and encouraging them to participate fully in the life of their community and church: www.stjoseph.org.uk

Through the Roof is a Christian disability charity that changes the lives of disabled people around the world and helps others to change lives too. They aim to ensure that everyone is valued equally and able to contribute their gifts and skills: www.throughtheroof.org

National Catholic Disability Partnership (USA): Working in faith, gift and partnerships with disabled people ensuring access to faith and community: www.ncpd.org

Further reading: disability theology

Brock, B. (ed.), *Disability in the Christian Tradition: a reader* (Michigan: Wm B. Eerdmans, 2012) pp. 1-100

Eiesland, N., *The Disabled God: toward a liberatory theology of disability* (Nashville: Abingdon Press, 1994)

Gangemi, C., and Waldron, L., *Intellectual Disabilities: caring for yourself and others* (Chawton: Redemptorist Publications, 2018)

Gaventa, W., *Disability and Spirituality: recovering wholeness* (Waco, Texas: Baylor University Press, 2018)

Matthews, P., *Pope John Paul II and the Apparently "Non-Acting" Person* (Herefordshire: Gracewing, 2013)

Matthews, P., *God's Wild Flowers* (Herefordshire: Gracewing, 2016)

Reinders, H., *Receiving the Gift of Friendship* (Michigan: Wm B. Eerdmans, 2008)

Swinton, J., *Becoming Friends of Time: disability, timefullness and gentle discipleship* (London: SCM Press, 2016)

Walmsley, J., and Johnson, K., *Inclusive Research with People with Learning Disabilities* (London: Jessica Kingsley Publishers, 2003)

Wyatt, J., *Matters of Life and Death: human dilemmas in the light of the Christian faith* (Nottingham: InterVarsity Press, 2009)

Articles

Badetti, L., "Self and Community: the importance of interdependence and its shadow side", *Journal of Disability and Religion*, vol. 20 (2016), no 3, pp. 154-162

Dillon, K., (2006) "The Spiritual Growth of People with Intellectual Disabilities: Jean Vanier and John of the Cross", doctoral thesis, Heythrop College, University of London (2006)

Gangemi, C., "The Word, Alive and at Work", *Journal of Disability and Religion* (16 August 2012), pp. 287-288

"Living Fully", special edition, *Cultura e Fede*, vol. XXIV (2016), no 3

Matthews, P., "Why Me?", conference paper of the 6th International Colloquium of the International Association of Catholic Bioethicists (2013)

Romero, M., "The Goodness and Beauty of our Fragile Flesh: principled avoidance", *Journal of Moral Theology*, vol. 6, Special Issue 2 (2017), p. 213

Swinton, J., (2011) "Who Is the God We Worship?", *International Journal of Pastoral Theology*, vol. 14 (2011), pp. 273-307

NOTES

1 Wyatt, J., *Matters of Life and Death: human dilemmas in the light of the Christian faith* (Nottingham: InterVarsity Press, 2009), p. 29.

2 Whitehead, J., and Whitehead, E., *Method in Ministry: theological reflection and Christian ministry* (London: Sheed & Ward, 1999), p. 9.

3 Gangemi, C., Tobanelli, M., Vincenzi, G., and Swinton, J., "EveryBody Has a Story: meeting people with intellectual disabilities and responding to their spiritual and religious needs", research project with University of Aberdeen, 2010.

4 Gangemi, Tobanelli, Vincenzi and Swinton, "EveryBody Has a Story".

5 *Scintilli* is an Italian word meaning "sparks" and is often used in prayer surrounding grace. It is pronounced "shintilly".

6 Pope Francis, *Gaudete et Exsultate*, 14.

7 In presenting the MEET process as a method for the book, I would like to acknowledge the influence of a "Method for Ministry", developed by Whitehead and Whitehead. It has guided my ministry and provided me with a "portable method" for bringing the three poles of theological reflection into conversation: Experience, Culture and Tradition. See Whitehead and Whitehead, *Method in Ministry*, p. 3.

8 In an important and insightful chapter in the book *Remorse and Reparation*, Baroness Sheila Hollins, a leading voice in psychiatry and intellectual disability, speaks about some of the psychological difficulties that people with disabilities might experience. Hollins suggests that "Perhaps if people feel that it is their fault that they are different, then they feel responsible for making amends." However, if it is not possible to make adequate reparation, "[because they are who they are, a person and not a medical condition] then they might expect to be punished for the rest of their lives by those who [seem] so burdened by their presence". Hollins suggests that this *possible* train of thought might explain some of the dysfunctional relationships with parents and carers by, and high risk of depression in, people with intellectual disabilities as well as some of the behaviour that might be challenging. See Hollins, S., "Remorse for Being: through the lens of learning disability", in Murray Cox, ed., *Remorse and Reparation* (London: Jessica Kingsley, 1998), p. 98.

9 Matthews, P., *Pope John Paul II and the Apparently "Non-Acting" Person* (Herefordshire: Gracewing, 2013), p. 93.

10 In West, C., *Theology of the Body Explained: a commentary on John Paul II's "gospel of the body"* (Herefordshire: Gracewing, 2003), p. 7.

11 Matthews, *Pope John Paul II and the Apparently "Non-Acting" Person*.

12 Haight, R., *The Experience and Language of Grace* (New Jersey: Paulist Press, 1979), p. 11.

13 Second Vatican Council, *Dei Verbum* (Dogmatic Constitution on Divine Revelation), 2, "In his goodness and wisdom God chose to reveal himself and to make known to us the hidden purpose of his will (see Eph. 1:9) by which through Christ, the Word made flesh, man might in the Holy Spirit have access to the Father and come to share in the divine nature (see Eph. 2:18; 2 Peter 1:4). Through this revelation, therefore, the invisible God (see Col. 1:15, 1 Tim. 1:17) out of the abundance of his love speaks to men as friends (see Ex. 33:11; John 15:14-15) and lives among them (see Bar. 3:38), so that he may invite and take them into fellowship with himself."

14 Karl Rahner, an influential theologian who has had a significant impact on contemporary theological thinking, identifies that "Love does not find its full realization out of its own resources but from the radical unity it has with the love of God in Jesus Christ." Karl Rahner, "The One Christ and the Universality of Salvation", *Theological Investigations* vol. 16 (New York: Crossroad, 1979), 223, in Masson, R., "Spirituality for the Head, Heart, Hands, and Feet: Rahner's Legacy", in *Spirituality Today*, Vol. 36 (Winter 1984), No. 4, pp. 340-54.

15 Matthews, P., *God's Wild Flowers* (Herefordshire: Gracewing, 2016), p. xiii.

16 Matthews, P., "Why Me?" Conference paper of the 6th International Colloquium of the IACB, 2013.

17 Address of Pope Francis to participants in the conference organised by the Pontifical Council for promoting New Evangelisation and Catechesis, Clementine Hall, 21 October 2017.

18 "Living Fully" statement, in *Cultura e Fede*, vol. XXIV (2016), no 3, p. 210.

19 Sullivan, W.F., and Heng, J., "People with Intellectual and Developmental Disabilities and their Families: an ethical framework and recommendations for health care practices and policies", consensus Statement of the 6th International Colloquium of the International Association of Catholic Bioethicists (IACB), in *The National Catholic Bioethics Quarterly*, vol. 15, issue 2 (2015) #23.

20 Assaf, A., *Pope Francis' Little Book of Wisdom* (London: HarperCollins, 2015), p. 191.

21 I would like to acknowledge the invaluable guidance of Agnes Rees in creating these guidelines.

22 Summary from *Guidelines for health professionals supporting families experiencing perinatal loss*, 2001, Canadian Paediatric Society ©all rights reserved.

23 Cahill, B., *Living with Grief: walking the spiral* (Chawton: Redemptorist Publications, 2015), p. 92.

24 Martin Lloyd Williams shares his personal reflections of the birth of his son with Down syndrome and the prayerful and ongoing reflection that he has undertaken with a painting by Andrea Mantegna, *The Presentation of the Christ Child*, in Lloyd Williams, M., *Beauty and Brokenness: compassion and the kingdom of God* (London: SPCK, 2007), p. 2.

25 Lloyd Williams, *Beauty and Brokenness*, p. 8.

26 Egan, D.H., "The Mystical Theology of Karl Rahner", *The Way* (April 2013), pp. 43-62, available at <https://theway.org.uk/Back/522Egan.pdf>

27 Gangemi, Tobanelli, Vincenzi and Swinton, "EveryBody Has a Story", p. 3, available from the author.

28 This is a very powerful story of a Christian couple in England who chose to continue with their pregnancy, knowing that their child would die immediately after birth. This beautiful and strikingly honest book tells of the journey of a family with their unborn daughter and sibling. Williams, S., *The Shaming of the Strong: the challenge of an unborn life* (Eastbourne: Kingsway, 2005).

29 *BIA* parents' resource. The principle of "loving their child for the whole of her/his life" is a way of helping parents reflect upon everything that they choose to do as an act of love. This is especially important in the life of a child who dies before, during or after birth. The issue of "loving for the whole of a lifetime" is explained in chapters 5, 6 and 7 of the *BIA* parents' resource.

30 Sgreccia, E., and Laffitte, J. (eds), *Alongside the Incurably Sick and Dying Person: ethical and practical aspects* (Vatican City: Libreria Editrice Vaticana, 2008), p. 244.

31 See n. 14 on the thinking of Karl Rahner on this matter.

32 Whitehead and Whitehead, *Method in Ministry*, p. 5.

33 Cameron, H., Bhatti, D., Duce, C., Sweeney, J., and Watkins, C., *Talking about God in Practice (London: SCM Press, 2010)*, p. 55.

34 Gangemi, C., and Waldron, L., *Intellectual Disability: caring for yourself and others* (Chawton: Redemptorist Publications, 2018), p. 33.

35 Comonsoli, Bishop Peter, "The celebration of the Christian mystery: sacraments as precious occasions for catechesis", conference paper, Rome, on the occasion of the conference with the Pontifical Council for the Promotion of Evangelisation; and "Catechesis and Persons with Disabilities: a necessary engagement in the life and mission of the Church", 21 October 2017, p. 3.

36 Comonsoli, p. 3.

37 Comonsoli, p.3.

38 Linn, S., Linn, D., and Linn, M., *Healing our Beginning* (New Jersey: Paulist Press, 2005), Kindle version.

39 Comonsoli, p. 3.

40 Donatello, V., Sr, "Pope Francis: The Gospel and Fraternity in Practice", conference paper on the occasion of the International Congress of the European Society of Catholic Theologians, "Philadelphia: the challenge of fraternity", 2 August 2017, Strasbourg, p. 3.

41 Matthews, P., "Life in Christ: the person made in the image of God", conference paper, Rome, on the occasion of the conference with the Pontifical Council for the Promotion of Evangelisation; and "Catechesis and Persons with Disabilities: a necessary engagement in the life and mission of the Church", 21 October 2017, p. 1.

42 Masters, A., "Don't Worry: he is in a perpetual state of grace", in "Living Fully", special edition, *Cultura e Fede*, vol. XXIV (2016), no 3, p. 186.

43 Musyima Kitaka, P., O.Carm., Homily for the third Sunday of Easter, Rome, 2018, p. 1.

44 Musyima Kitaka, p. 1.

45 Musyima Kitaka, p. 1.

46 Haight, *The Experience and Language of Grace*, p. 21.

47 Swinton, J., *Becoming Friends of Time: disability, timefullness and gentle discipleship* (London: SCM Press, 2016), p. 208.

48 Matthews, P., "The Wonder of Me: disability and Pope John Paul II's theology of the body", in "Living Fully", special edition, *Cultura e Fede*, vol. XXIV (2016), no 3, p. 183.

49 Reinders, H., "Seeing with the Eyes of God", in "Living Fully", special edition, *Cultura e Fede*, vol. XXIV (2016), no 3, p. 182.

50 Gaventa, W., *Disability and Spirituality: recovering wholeness* (Waco, Texas: Baylor University Press, 2018), p. 283.

51 Badetti, L., "Self and Community: the importance of interdependence and its shadow side", *Journal of Disability and Religion,* vol. 20 (2016), no. 3, p. 161.

52 *Discorso 24.VII.2013*, in Caruana, E., and Tagliaferri, L., *Un Abbraccio Di Speranza Pensieri di Papa Francesco ai malati* (Vatican: Libreria editrice vaticano, 2017), p. 7.

53 The people in the image witness to the potential in life. I would like to thank my colleague theologian Sarah Long, who is delivering her doctoral thesis on disability and theology to Pope Francis.

54 This prayer came from a reflection with Fr Míceál O'Neill O.Carm., prior of Centro Internazionale Sant'Alberto, Rome. It is based on his study of Santa Maddalena De Pazzi, a Florentine Carmelite

nun, who also reflected upon the life of the unborn Christ, *Cantico per l'Amore non amato* (Comunita di San Leolino, 2016).

55 Gaventa, B. (23 June 2016), "Hidden in Plain Sight."

56 Reinders, J. (23 June 2016), Symposium introduction, "Seeing With the Eyes of God."

57 Masters, "Don't Worry". The use of the plural of persons and disabilities in the reference, "persons with disabilities" is a theological reference that points to the uniqueness of each person, as well as the variability of the experience of disability. This is to counter the perception that individuals with disabilities share the same characteristics, concerns and experiences of disability.

58 Long, S. (24 June 2016), "This is Me."

59 Pontifical Council for Culture (1999), "Towards a Pastoral Approach to Culture" (TPAC) <http://www.vatican.va/roman_curia/pontifical_councils/cultr/documents/rc_pc_pc-cultr_doc_03061999_pastoral_en.html>

60 "Towards a Pastoral Approach to Culture", para. 1, citing Pope John Paul II in FN 1, *Discours à l'Assemblée Générale des Nations Unies*, 5 October 1995, n. 9; *Documentation Catholique*, XCII (1995) 920. <http://www.vatican.va/roman_curia/pontifical_councils/cultr/documents/rc_pc_pc-cultr_doc_03061999_pastoral_en.html>

61 Long. S (2016); Reinders, J. (2016).

62 Reinders, J. (2016); Romero, M. (24 June 2016), "When We See Servulus: learning how to go on by looking to the past."

63 Braviner, B., and Lucas, D. (23 June 2016), "The Jesus Model: the person with disabilities and the disabled God."

64 Pope Francis (11 June 2016), Address for the 25th Anniversary of the Concillio Episcopale Italiana (CEI), Disability Ministry; Sr Veronica Donatello, Don Diego Pancaldo e Sr. Antonella Meneghetti (CEI) (23 June 2016), "O Tutti, O Nessuno."

65 Pope Francis (11/6/16).

66 Pope Francis (11/6/16).

67 Cardinal Gianfranco Ravasi (23/6/16), Opening address of Living Fully 2016 Academic symposium 23 June 2016.

68 Ravasi, Opening address.

69 Matthews, P. (24/6/16), "The Wonder of Who I Am."

70 Collectively reported in the papers and insights of all delegates, presenters and facilitators at Living Fully 2016.

71 Masters, A. (23/6/16).

72 Based on Living Fully 2016 papers: Long, S. (2016); Masters (23/6/16); Waldron, L. (24/6/16) "Issues of Disability, Loneliness and Isolation."

73 Gangemi, C. (24/6/16), quoting Canon J. O'Toole. (July 2014), Homily for ongoing formation of priests, Southwark.

74 Matthews, P. (2016).

75 Reinders, J. (2016).

76 Pope Francis (11/6/16).

77 Matthews, P. (2016).

78 Reinders, J. (2016).

79 Dukes, Z. (25/6/16), "From Inclusion to Belonging: navigating a way forward."

80 Romero, M. (2016); Pope Francis (11/6/2016).

81 Gangemi, Tobanelli, Vincenzi and Swinton (2010). The term "EveryBody" was developed by the research project "EveryBody Has A Story: meeting people with intellectual disability" and responding to their spiritual and religious needs (available from the author).

82 Gill, P. (2016), review document and Rae, E., "A Quest to Belong."

83 Henley, C. (2016), "Ask Not What the Church Can Offer."

84 FitzSimons, J. (2016), Conference discussion.

85 "'Love the Lord your God with all your heart, with all your soul, with all your mind and with all your strength.' The second is this: 'You must love your neighbour as yourself.' There is no commandment greater than these."

86 Walsh, M.B. (23/6/16), "Autism, Culture, Church: from disruption to hope."

87 Demeter, D. (23/6/16), "Mental Obstacle Clearing."

88 Montali, M., and Orso, L. (23/6/16), "MS Network: a way out of isolation."

89 Bishop Paul Hendricks (26/6/16), closing address Living Fully 2016.

90 This was a common theme, highlighted in all papers and reflections of delegates.

91 Delegate (26/6/16), "Creating a Charter for the Church."

92 Pope Francis (11/6/16).

93 Legal rights here refer to responsibilities placed on the Church by disability legislation in certain countries.

94 Reinders, J. (2016); Gaventa, B. (2016) and statement contribution.

95 This was a collective message from all delegates and presenters at Living Fully 2016 events.

96 Townsend, M. (26/6/16), Statement workshop.

97 Masters, A. (25/6/16), Gathering Stories: "A Church Called to Love."

98 Dukes, Z. (2016).

99 Rooney, S., and Grant, F. (24/6/16), "In From the Wilderness."

100 Pope Francis (11/6/16).

101 Mike Harris, specialist in symbolic and differentiated communication, summarising discussions in Stream A.

102 Julia FitzSimons, Stream A facilitator.

103 Pope Francis (11/6/16).

104 Pope Francis (11/6/16).

105 Ray, M. (26/6/16), Statement workshop.

106 Vuk, M. (23/6/16), "Friendship with People with Disabilities – Ideal or Reality."

107 We acknowledge with thanks the contribution of the Livability charity in encouraging us to use aspects of their charter for change as a model and guide.